Pilgr

an anthology of Christian verse

sponsored by Feather Books
selected and edited by Walter Nash

Published by Feather Books
PO Box 438
Shrewsbury SY3 0WN, UK
Tel/fax; 01743 872177

Website URL: http://www.waddysweb.freeuk.com
e-mail: john@waddysweb.freeuk.com

Feather Books wishes to thank
Josie Davies
for her cover illustration

ISBN-10:   1-84175-224-X
ISBN-13: 978-1-84175-224-2

First published 2006

No. 240 in the Feather Books Poetry Series

For advice sought and generously given, we wish to thank
Roger Kojecky, editor of *The Glass*

Foreword by Revd John Waddington-Feather

It gives me great pleasure, as editor of Feather Books and the Poetry Church magazine, to sponsor *Pilgrimages*, an anthology of Christian poems published under the imprint of this press. For Walter Nash, its compiler, this has been a welcome task, yet one not without problems, since the process of selection has necessarily involved the rejection of many good poems, equal in Christian worth to the finally chosen texts. Without this company of the unselected, our magazine would cease to exist, for it is their poetry the makes up the quarterly issues of Poetry Church.

It began life in 1995, when a group of poets approached me as director of Feather Books and asked me to launch a specifically Christian poetry magazine, as they couldn't get their work published in the small secular magazines. At that time, there was – and still is – an unwillingness to publish religious verse whatever its quality. Publishing, like everything else, was affected by postmodernism – the movement of anti-religion and anarchy of the 1980s which has affected all sections of western thinking, including poetry.

From the start *Poetry Church* had a pastoral role as well as a literary one, and it has always been ecumenical. Some of its poets suffer chronic illness and are housebound; others are long-term prisoners introduced to the magazine by contributors and its editor, an honorary prison chaplain of many years' standing. An early contributor to the magazine was Sean Sellars, a young poet on Death Row in Oklahoma Penitentiary. Tragically, he was executed in 1999, but sent us some fine poems and valued greatly the correspondence he had with fellow poets and the prayers for him the eleven years he was on Death Row from the age of fifteen.

The first number of *Poetry Church* was published early in 1996. It was very simply produced and was only 14 pages long. It circulated to around 30 subscribers in England, whose subscriptions just about paid for its publication. Today, it is 40 pages long, well produced, and is distributed internationally to over 300 subscribers. It goes free to those who can't afford the subscription like our poets in prison.

Walter Nash, Emeritus Professor of English at Nottingham University, joined us early in 1998. He also introduced other academics to the magazine and now there is a caucus of professors and lecturers supporting its ventures. As a result, its contents cover a very wide range of poetry and in the last nine years Feather Books has published almost 300 private collections of verse by poets all over the world. I ought to add, too, that Professor Nash has been pivotal in the encouraging and editing the work of a group of 'Poetry Churchers' all past their three score and ten years. This has been one of the remarkable features of the magazine, that is has 'called forth' poetic talent in this elderly (?) group, many of them gifted women poets and poets like Laurie Bates to whom this anthology is dedicated.

Small press magazines are often one-man or one-woman ventures. Among them, the magazines of Jon Silkin, Howard Sergeant, Eric Ratcliffe, Gerald England, Mabel Ferrett, Vera Rich, Joan Lee – all pioneers of successful magazines. But I would like to think that *Poetry Church* is rather different, a fellowship of Christians, which I hope will continue for many years after its present editor has laid down his pen here, and hopefully is editing and writing in more ethereal realms.

Contents

INTRODUCTION, by Walter Nash

I. The Light Breaks Through

II. Desperations

III. My Father's House

IV These Thy Servants

V. Theologies

VI.   <u>**Comings and Gainrisings**</u>

VII Mythologies

VIII Images and Words

IX Christian Occasions

X All Things Bright And Beautiful

XI **Something For The Journey**

XII Closing the Book

INDEX OF POETS AND POEMS

Pilgrimages: An Anthology of Christian Verse

Introduction by Walter Nash

The verses in this collection are the work of a company of poets who are, figuratively, the "parishioners" of John Waddington-Feather – in his time variously priest, paratrooper, pugilist, protector of the poor, poet, and latterly publisher, the founder of a small press called Feather Books, and the editor of a quarterly magazine, *Poetry Church*. All the poets represented here have been contributors to that magazine, and some – the core of the anthology – have published substantial collections in the Feather Books Poetry Series. For this volume I have selected 176 poems, sifting and sampling through *Poetry Church* in its seasonal and annual issues from over the past decade, and some 40 chapbook collections from the same period. It has been a pleasant labour, but one that has obliged me to ask, more than occasionally, a serious question. What, after all, makes a poem "Christian", or "religious" – apart from the company it keeps, which is not a negligible qualification?

There are poems here that in themselves might seem committed to nothing, except in the way that a negative is committed to a photograph, as a dark prefiguring of light. Andrew Challen's *A Weekend Drinks Party* [7], William Rowell's *Shoe* [12], are two examples of poems that have, certainly, a "moral pressure", but may not appear to be essentially religious. Yet here, because of the company they are obliged to keep, in editorial categories guided by a compiler's hand, they are felt religiously. They are not religious poems of a kind that is packed with doctrine and devotion, glorifying the name of

God and the fellowship of Christ; nor are they of a sort that deals so discreetly with religious inference as to make hints in a brief word or phrase that becomes the secret index to the poem. (Try *A.N.Other* [59], or *Where You Are* [58], where the very last word of the poem is the defining cue) The poems I mean carry no such indicative mark. They involve the reader intuitively, in perceiving a predisposition or "mind-set" in the writer; the reader thus has an option, as co-author of the poem, a maker creating his own perceptions in what another has made. Why should I read Josie Davies' *Almost You* [64] as a poem about the possibly risen Christ, when it seems pretty clearly to be a poem about lost love? And if I am to take Laurie Bates' *Bold and Brave* [152] as a precise and sympathetic documentation of a street scene, with a hint by the way for the Social Services Dept., why need I feel in it the shadow-presence of something more, something like Bethlehem, the inn, the manger, Mother and Child? There is nothing in the text so obvious for these connections to be inescapable; but for me, as a Christian, all the facts of the poem cluster to a shadowed meaning.

A medieval exegete, following the master, Thomas Aquinas, would have taken it for granted that a meaningful text has both a literal and a spiritual meaning, and that the two kinds are involved in each other. The literal is the ascertainable fact of the text, in its wording, its grammar, its metaphor and rhetoric – the business of the commentator being to establish, through close reading, *what the text really says*; beyond that, though prefigured in that, lie the spiritual senses that constitute *what the text really means*. Now the medieval commentators were dissecting Holy Writ, the Scriptures, which they took for truth compounded of truths, and we are not entitled to claim that kind of status for our poems. Nevertheless, there is much of the present collection to engage us with layers of meaning, and to suggest that poetry can be read "at different levels", an effect of poetic truth in the service of divine truth, a manifest of "words that touch on the Word's forever unspoken fact". The poems frequently imply an allegorical significance, or invoke a *tropology*, a moral application, or do both of those things at once, while the reader muses over the literal text.

The poems are ordered here as a narrative, or "argument" in twelve sections, following phases of Christian experience, as evoked by the section headings. This arrangement was not preconceived; it happened, during the collection of the poems, that they assigned themselves quite readily to some persistent and definable themes. So the opening section is a celebration of light breaking out of darkness; the second, a counter-theme, of desperation, of barrenness, of suspicion and fear, fear even of the adumbrated presences of hope. The third section speaks of the church, not the Church-in-the-grand-abstract, but a solid, local, seemly house, a "home", in Robert Frost's sense of "home" as "a place where, when you have to go there, they have to let you in". This leads to section IV, These Thy Servants, which evokes, not without humour, the characters of ecclesiastical shepherds and the needy longings of their sheep. Section V, called Theologies dwells on some of the longings the pulpit does not quite assuage. It represents individuals trying to answer their own obsessively unanswerable questions, about the purpose of life, the reality of experience, the introversions of the mind, the lapses of the heart – to frame, in short, their personal theologies.

In VII, Comings and Gainrisings, there is but one question, "When will Christ come again?" with the rider, "And how?" In "Gainrising" (that lovely word invented by Sir John Cheke, who taught Greek but advocated Saxon usages) the poems speak in two minds, reverent or sceptical; about the Gainrising. Josie Davies' *Almost You* [64] speaks in tender hesitancy of the risen Christ, glimpsed in the street and immediately lost to view; but William Ruleman's brilliantly satirical *A Second Coming* [66] casts the Saviour as the helpless victim of ruthless commercial interests. These inventions are born out of the poets' preoccupation with the idea of Christ's re-entry into a culture like ours. Invention, however, or call it devout speculation, is a liberty allowed to the Christian poet. That we freely invent or elaborate our own versions of the personalities and motives of Biblical figures, appears from VII, Mythologies, devoted to scriptural story-telling. This is not to use "myth" with the vulgar, newspaper imputation of "falsehood", but rather in the sense of "explanatory narrative". Some of the characters "explained" here are Biblical figures, but others have no scriptural warrant at all, except as inferred existences; for example *Bathsheba's Maid*, in Joan Sheridan Smith's poem of that name [71], or the woman Isabella Strachan has called *The Governor's Wife* [79]. Such poems undoubtedly have a religious stance to convey – they have, so to speak, their tropology – but they are also accomplished examples of the story-teller's art.

Religious art is the theme of section VIII, Images and Words, where the poems are about artefacts and their inner significance, or about makers (artists) creating poems, paintings, prayers. Here, a poem of high art is Caroline Glyn's *Caedmon* [88], expansively based on the Venerable Bede's tale about the unmusical cowherd who woke one morning to find himself in possession of a unique gift of song. It celebrates the idea of divine inspiration, or an empowering above one's usual powers. On the other hand, Idris Caffrey's little poem *Street Players* [92] wryly dismisses the idea of the inspired artist creating works that will last for ever. God comes into the poem as "another unseen who claps silently", but knows that the show will last for no more than a mortal day.

Section IX, <u>Christian Occasions</u>, contains no moment of dissent or counterpoise, the poems marking, like so many calendar entries, events in the religious year, from Advent, through Christmas, Epiphany, Candlemas, Lady Day, Lent, Easter, Pentecost. The poems in general affirm the scripture and rejoice in it. Only in *The Crucifiers* [112] and *On the Via Dolorosa* [113] is there a distancing note, not of disbelief, but of rueful irony, as the poet views the brutal long-ago Easter happening in a modern perspective implying the unaltered but cryptic brutality of the present. Occasions of a different sort are celebrated in X, <u>Natural Histories</u>. Some people are brought to God via the lectern and pulpit; some by neighbourly example; many make the transition through sheer delight in the physical world, its plants and trees, its creatures, even its household furnishings or garden plots – for the latter, see Lauries Bates' exquisite lyric *The Pool* [134]; others again simply find in nature the images that express their religious perceptions. Martin Linford's <u>Grace</u> [116] is the poem that best expresses this garden-drift to redemption; but Susan Glyn's more complex, restive poem *At The Air Show* [130] proposes a way to grace through "the dream of flying" like wheeling birds, into the circuit of infinity. There are many moods of revelation through nature – even the experience of swimming with dolphins (see Philip Comfort's *dolphin dawn* [132])

The tenor of section XI, <u>Something For The Journey</u> was suggested by another of Susan Glyn's reflections on man among his mechanisms, *Trans-Europe Express* [145], which ends with the line "Nothing belongs to you – except the ride" This is a section for meditations by the way: on persons encountered, on lessons learned, on regrets, on friendship and marriage, on memories, on "the ride" in all its hopeful uncertainty. In the penultimate poem in this section, *Love* [163], Laurie Bates speaks, with characteristic unflinching honesty, of "the quest for what we do not know / and may not be found / this side the grave – or beyond." And so section XII , <u>Closing the Book</u>, looks "this side and beyond the grave". Closing the book means ending the story; it also means settling accounts. Pamela Constantine's splendid *The Prodigal* [167] tells of the soul coming to repentant terms with its predicament. William Ruleman's *One Recent Summer* [169] speaks of humanity unamended. The mood in these latterday poems is one of resignation, confession, some apprehension, but also of hope, nobly expressed by Bruce James's *In What Deep of Love* [174], concisely fixed in Caroline Glyn's *Jerusalem* [175], where the final light of hope is caught as in the facets of a jewel. In the concluding *Prayer* [176], Bruce James speaks simply, submissively, not in the style of the magniloquent poet, his usual vein, but as one making halting petition for us all.

In each section, the constituent poems are ordered, now for similarity, now for contrast, but mostly in the hope that the poems will seem to "speak" to each other, their dialogue filling the imagined space of a section as delegates fill a conference room with their discussions, arguments, proposals, points of order. Some of the delegates belong in more than one room, but I have made the choice for them, whether effectively or inanely only the readers of the anthology can say. As for the poets in conference, these are people worth getting to know, gifted in their perceptions and enjoying their considerable share of technical ability. "For nimble tongues and lame have both found favour", says Auden, not referring to religion, but to something serviceable to religion, the poet's art. Not that there are many lame tongues in this assembly. I have lost track of the poetic forms, so adroitly managed, which I have come across during my browsing, forms traditional or "free", though rarely so free as to be "innovative" to the point of being meaningless in a kind currently sought by some poetry magazines. But the contributors to this anthology have ambitions that preclude mere innovation; ambitions captured in the Psalmist's words: *"Thy statutes have been my songs in the house of my pilgrimage."* (Psalm 119, v.54)

Walter Nash

I. The Light Breaks Through

1. THE STILLNESS OF THE NIGHT

In the night,
how silent still and peaceful
as I lie quiet:
not aware I am awake until
small sounds recall.

There is the noise
of the far away friendly train,
as it comes and goes;
with that different sound for rain,
louder and deeper tone.

Away in the dark
in the wild wolf world outside,
a dog begins to bark
hollowly, to show he is on guard;
or perhaps afraid.

All at once a crack
loud inside the keyed-up house,
wooden, arthritic,
as if a joint stiff from disuse
moved for greater ease.

The silence profound
becomes absolute and solemn
a breath the only sound;
and I realise it is my own
and I lie down alone.

Laurie Bates

2. DARK NIGHT

I have no clear sight, except it be at night,
When the room is filled with inexplicable
            dark light;
Nor understanding, till in my mind is nothing,
And my heart feels so still that it seems
            no more living.

My greatest elation is the exultation
That follows five hours' silence and desolation.
Each night I lie in darkness and I die
A true death, when at last I cease to be I.

In the dark hours shine the consuming fires.
The flame is turning my body to ash as it
            devours.
When there is no more heat, a last death I
            shall meet,
My transformation and my joy then finally
            complete.

Caroline Glyn

3. INCARNATION

When the nightlight is first lit,
its spark is in danger from the wax
whose grossness can drown the fire.
Its little flame flickers alone
and the candle is dark.

As the flame hollows out the wax
and sinks below its rim,
we no longer see its brightness
but the radiance of incarnation
as the wax itself glows
translucent and finding its beauty
through the indwelling light.

Susan Glyn

4. EARTHRISE SUN

I caught the earthrise sun this morning
    in a slit between two sheaths of clouds
one hanging on the water like a lover
    the other hanging from the sky like a thief.
As the sun passed through these, it lingered
    just long enough in between to mean something.
I snatched this sign and ran it to the sea
    where I surfed the day by waves by storm,
as ghosts of water fell on breaks and peaks
    turning them velvet, soft, supple, sheen.
While thunder hollered on the hazed horizon,
    I slid down smooth silver cresting peaks
and joined our Creator, as rain from heaven
    dropped oceans and surfers mounted seas.

Philip Wesley Comfort

5. THE LIGHT

("The light shineth in darkness, and
the darkness comprehended it not."
John 1:5)

The light breaks through
clear as the sun's
gleam on a coffin-plate:

shouts from the open
bills of thrushes singing
through blossoms above a grave:

escapes from clenched
jaws that utter forgiveness
to mystified tormentors.

That light is the fifth
column that undermines
fragile empires of Hell:

dangerous secret
volcano that explodes
from unsuspecting darkness.

Robert Irwin

6. LIGHT AND LITANY

Turn about and walk away from the light,
leave candlelight electric light and daylight
and the organ's diminuendos;
pass stands of flowers chaste and white
and slanted shafts of Sunday sunlight
rainbowed through stained glass of gospel windows;
and almost blind with light come thankful home
to amber gleam of pews and honey-coloured stone,
and faces of friends hidden in hand and shadows.

Walk back from the light with your private face
eroded by years and wars, by cares and fears;
take off their rosy glasses and your false halo,
you have the callow look of fisted clay,
the medieval mason's crude wistful effigy
of common humanness that is your fellow;
gargoyles yearn in air, weep and wear
their stony hearts away, and though we shed no tear,
we also grieve who know we fall so far below.

Even thus unworthily, led by light and litany
and kneeling meekly, attend this Mystery.
Our secrets He knows and merciful has forgiven
us whose believing, for all our mind and might,
lies leaden and does not rise from the heart.
For poverty of soul there is no leaven
but kneel, kneel in hope – here are no alibis,
no winners, no losers, no failures, no lies.
His house has many rooms: Take heart, Everyman!

Laurie Bates

II. Desperations

7. A WEEKEND DRINKS PARTY

I was bidden to arrive before noon, and tried to do so,
First clambering into a good suit and clean shirt and so on,
Taking the tube, clutching a wrapped bottle of reasonable Spanish
Knowing that the other travellers thought my plumage 'over the top'.

I arrived and heard the chattering from outside the block:
"Darling! So nice to see you, and so formal, too!"
"Andrew, old son! Thanks for the contribution.
Have a drink and go on inside. Everyone's here."

I circulated, smiled at some and nodded to others.
I saw those I admired, or liked, (or detested)
I attempted idle conversation (which I know I do badly),
Even so I was aware I would be invited again.

I nibbled a sausage and passed round someone else's bottle.
I heard of holidays, then of children, and then of school fees,
Followed by gossip of whose adultery and whose money problems
And of whose latest 'success' and of whose newest 'disaster'.

I also heard about an old school-fellow and former colleague
Whose wife had acquired an appalling and incurable illness:
"Oh yeah. Chris. Nice chap. Pity about the wife!" Followed by
"Another drink! Go on! Twist your arm, eh?"

I asked for the loo, collected my brolly and left on tiptoe.

A.B.Challen

8. A LULL IN THE BATTLE

It's nearing midnight. Slowly the world's winding down.
A car droned past a moment ago, and rain-
drops tap the metal porch roof. I guess I'm sane,
and sane, for now, this sleepy little town
where a few dogs bark, and night is cloaked in a gown
of fog, and crickets chime, and surely no pain
is felt by anyone. Raising Cain
on a Sunday night is not our style. We frown
on Sabbath sensations. But come tomorrow morn,
we rev up our engines again, resume the race
for the fruit that will make us the apple of His eye.
All of our songs, the mad sun, and our glances warn
ourselves and others not to slacken our pace.
We know that some will fly, and some will die,
and none of us ever stops to question why.

William Ruleman

9. COMMON MAN

Those bumpkins
will be the death of me
with their hair like frightened straw;
wrenching words
out of their sockets.
Slow as snails
with that creature's preoccupations.
Nevertheless,
you can disarm them with a wink
and they are grateful for a smile,
like me.

John Cockle

10. CHANGED PRIORITIES

"Quick, they're knocking down the chapel."
We raced down the street,
 swerved at the corner shop
 and arrived breathless within a minute.
There was no need to have rushed –
 the workmen were just standing around
 gaping up at the grey silent stones
 as if they were waiting for God.

"Hey Mister, will you be using dynamite sticks?"
They started taking the building down
 bit by bit, stripping out anything of value
 so lead, wood and the organ went in on the lorry –
 prayer books and bibles into the skip.

"You kids clear off, now or you'll get hurt."
We'd soon lost interest anyway,
 headed off for the park to play,
 but every day as I walked past
 I looked through rusty railings,
 searched for angels in the tall grass.
After a week there was nothing left,
 an empty space returned again to the sky.

"You know that you have to pay here, mate?"
I park in a place where pews once stood,
 put silver coins into the collection box
 and can't help uttering a small prayer
 for this age we live in and old time's sake.

Idris Caffrey

11. HELL

We, each of us, make our own hell
And we do it deceiving no-one but ourselves
By first deciding just what it is we want:
Some ordinary ambition to thereby overwhelm our fancy,
Before becoming (all too easily) full-blown obsession,
As (unnoticed) it prises us from sense of proportion,
Our ordinary ambition now the worst sort of tyrant.

We, each of us, make our own hell
And we do it deceiving no-one but ourselves:
Our secret fears to be the bottomless pit
Which we mesmerise ourselves into jumping,
So determined are we to satiate that hunger
Which is the dread we ourselves made our master,
By first deciding just what it is we want.

A.B.Challen

12. SHOE

. . . . first light and sparrow-chatter:
under shadowed walls a discarded
          shoe lies half-hidden
          in the autumn tangle of weeds;
and that tyre tread burnt onto the pavement edge
          might attract a practised eye:
someone left here quickly.

the city wakes
          to rain streaking the dirty windows
          of the early buses,
a ritual sounding of horns,
the shouts of the early traders
          and the creak of their barrows;
like any morning; life going on.

and while tears blind the face
          behind those peeling shutters,
below the crawling urban river
          reflects in grey the
          unmarked, anonymous sky
                    and it's
          best not to know too much.

William Rowell

13. FAMILY MEAL

'So' she said, 'it's Sunday.
What do you fancy
for dinner today?

It's quick and easy
on the Motorway,
but noisy and so busy.

And Sunday's traditional,
something more suitable,
a nice family meal.'

'Well then, Maggie,' he says,
'traditional it is.
Robin would be nice.

I know a nest nearby
that we could try,
about ready to fly.

There's only the risk
the cat's been first,
so I'd better be brisk.

Leave it to me.
It'll be family,
just right for a Sunday.'

Laurie Bates

14. COULDN'T MAKE IT OUT

the bombs are falling in Baghdad.
our plane to Hawaii shut down.
terrorists are rousing their religion.
the Atlantic is storming furiously.

I couldn't make it out

I tried to push against the crazy waves.
even the young men were defeated.
the wind wins, always the wind.
whether it's over the ocean or sands.

they couldn't make it out

the bombs keep falling in Baghdad.
bodies fall over. Empires fall over.
whether evil or good. the wind wins.
always the wind over the ocean and sands.

no, I couldn't make it out

slim dictators rise and fall. governments
push hard and pall. the waves mount, plunge,
storm the sands. the victory is the sea's.
the wind is strong. stronger than any man.

no, I haven't made it out

the waves wash over the sands.
the winds wash over their bodies.
always the winds. always the waters.
and those who try to make it out.

Philip Wesley Comfort

15. AND WHO ARE YOU?

And who are you
in cold and grey,
shuffling in silence,
listening but not speaking,
tired and alone?

We are the ones
from the dark place
where you have never been,
beyond what you see or feel
or where you wish to go.

And who are you
that do not fit,
who stand aside
to make us feel uneasy,
and see what we could become?

We are the ones
who have never been
what you are,
and no longer
walk the paths you do.

And who are you
to watch and wait
and make us feel
obligation and debt
to ease your way?

We are the ones
who measure you
to chart your stride
on this world
and beyond.

M. Bedford

16. THE STRANGE PEOPLE

Don't look now, child,
for the Strange People are in town.
Ragtag and grumbly, they lope and limp
Across the square.

Look down at your feet, child,
their world has nothing to do with ours.
They have a different kind of thinking,
their minds are like their shoes,
scuffy and inward-turned,
hobbled and hesitant.

And don't you stare, child,
don't catch their frowny eyes,
don't match their silly smiles.
You don't want to know.
You really do not want to know.

But there's no need to worry, child,
they won't be here long;
twice round the market stalls, that's all,
with their gangly limbs and flapping coats
and their voices just too loud.

They will soon go back, child,
they will soon go
back to their parallel planet,
to the place where we can leave them,
safely out of mind,
out of sight;
no, they won't be here long.

Don't look now, child,
for the Strange People are in town.

William Rowell

III. My Father's House

17. PASSING THOUGHT

Occasionally as I see a church
I just 'pop in' and pay a little visit,
So at that final count,
When I am carried in,
God won't ask, "Whoever is it?"

Duncan Robson

18. ONCE AGAIN

Sometimes we suddenly see things
that for too long have been away.

Through tall tangled trees
I make out the church again -
black as a crow rising to meet morning.
Maybe it was the patch of red
flaming behind its ancient presence
that drew my gaze as the cold wind came,
cut thin by its slanted towers.

Whatever it was I stumble towards
the oak doors, where I wonder
if perhaps today God has painted
a different kind of sky because He knows
in this age, we are drawn to strange things
and with half an eye may discover
that place where we can begin to find Him.

Idris Caffrey

19. FORTY THOUSAND DAYS

The church is closed —
boarded up against
those who never came,
but now want to play
the organ and set fire
to the pulpit for a laugh.

A hundred years
locked away to the dark,
while on the other side of the street
our lives go hurrying past.

Idris Caffrey

20. ST PETER'S CHURCH , BROMYARD

The long, low pile of Peter Church,
Sunk below the grass on graves,
As a ship moored to the hard
Half knows the town, and half the waves.
Step down and feel your feet
Freed from the need to walk
A journey more this week,
Or seek another gain.

Now the nave resounds to Easter praise,
Protected from the glare, this cosy light
Is Spring distilled for us to sip and save,
Blooms protected from the blight,
Love within the walls that chases out
Envy and evasion, even hate.

Hugh Hellicar

21. ST NON'S, PEMBROKE

Outside, the raven croaks
Over the steady splash of waves on rocks
Below the well and grassy garth,
Where David's mother gave him birth
Within the circling ancient stones,
Amid the fury of the crashing storms.

Within, the sheltered space,
The scented warmth and glowing grace
Of waxy candles, falls
Silently, across the rough-hewn walls –
The stones retrieved, reprieved, the yield
From ruined chapel in the field.

Beyond, the buzzards mew
And glide, above the living bleeding yew,
Over the graves and holy cross-
Still whirling round a central boss,
With coils and circles yet displayed
Beneath the mount where Brynach prayed.

Inside, the sunlight weaves
About the knotted stone beneath the eaves
Which sainted Brynach carried here –
A friendship gift from David, where
The twisted strands of destiny
Unite all life in woven harmony.

Tina Negus

[Ed: St David of Wales, the son of King Sant/Prince Sandde of Ceredigion, and the
Lady Nonna, or St Non, was born in the protective circle of a howling storm, on a
sea head in Prmbrokeshire. The place is now called St David's. Nonna built a chapel
there, the ruins of which can still be seen. This chapel was restored and rededicated
by a Roman Catholic Order, the Passionist Fathers, in 1951.]

22. ST EDEYRN'S CHURCH, CARDIFF

This place has patiently
rolled with history's punches.
The Conqueror's men, Glyndwr's
and Cromwell's have shouted past,
or left their bits of graffiti.

Like small unnoticed Kilroys
others have left signs
of quieter passings. Prayers
pack every cranny and niche –
a magazine piled high

with kegs of prayer. If sudden
destruction smashed these walls,
you feel the lot might explode
in fall-out clouds of grace
to dress the wounds of the earth.

Robert Irwin

[Ed: Glyndwr, anglice Glendower. "Kilroy" in allusion to the wartime graffito, "Kilroy was here". Kilroy was the American version of the observant wanderer.. The British equivalent was called Chad. His bald head peered over a wall, with a plus and minus for eyes; in fact, he was a rudimentary circuit diagram. The Anglo-Saxons called him Widsith, meaning "Far-travelled" – as in the Homeric epithet for Odysseus, *polytropos*]

23. SUNDAY AFTERNOON IN HOLY TRINITY CHURCH

Cold afternoon in June.
People drift into church,
admire memorial tablets,
the carved wooden rood-screen,
angels on the roof,
and the Victorian stained glass.

A few linger in the prayer corner.
Nobody speaks above a whisper.
Sometimes a child's voice
breaks the silence.

We're here
just to see that nothing's stolen
or broken. History is all around:
The Clifford tombs, the mediaeval pillars,
the Castle just next door.

I suppose most visitors come in like Larkin.
They read the leaflets thoughtfully supplied
by the Parish Council. Then they drop a coin
in the collecting box.

Joan Sheridan Smith

[Ed: The church is in Skipton, Yorkshire. Of the ancient family of the Cliffords, Joan Sheridan Smith has written in her sonnet sequence, <u>Lady Anne's Quire</u> (Poetry Monthly Press, Nottingham, 2000). The Larkin reference is to his poem, "Church Going". She is perhaps a little unjust to the church visitor in that poem, who, in Goldsmith's phrase, "came to scoff but remained to pray".

24. FOUNTAINS ABBEY

Even the skeleton is impressive,
enough is there to furnish conjecture
of the whole colossal structure.
Arched ribs surround the heart in massive

stone, not bone. This is no dinosaur,
although it seems as obsolete.
But try with the mind's eye
to see again this forest filled with song.

For all the floodlights and the scaffolding,
uneasy jokes to chip solemnity
or cameras winking at the cheerful sun,
you'll not dispel the Presence that is there.

The empty arches lift their hands in prayer.

Joan Sheridan Smith

25. YORK MINSTER SPEAKS

I cloak in storm-cloud,
violet on violet;
splitting-sky lightening
sprites upward,
orange and blue.
I am unafraid;
Having the ear of God.

Time passes.
Standing dry and cool,
I am cathedral.
The cloud has changed her robe
shielding sun with rose.

Thelma Laycock

26. LADY CHAPEL

Pink and rosy Portland stone,
light behind the ancient glass,
chiaroscuroed, tiled floor,
ochre tablet, golden brass.

Laurel wreaths a crown of thorns,
trug of willow, wand of youth;
by the altar, nettle crowns,
lily's coolness, poppy's truth.

Gentle Joseph looking down,
King of heaven, Lord of earth,
stillest child, without a sound,
frozen at this point of birth.

Kingdom's votive candles cast,
shades of shadow, light and flame,
holding back our darker place,
flashes incandescent, reigns.

Lady, He the light I seek,
hold Him safe, my precious Lord,
so we lose, like you, to win,
in that loss ourselves restored.

Paul Beatty

27. THE LINGUA FRANCA

For when we enter their ambiance
that fair, not far, not foreign place,
we could embrace the good people,
the joyful peaceful way of life,
what we would call Christian,
for they smile and we feel so welcome:
not to complain, the only problem is
we hear them speak, but what they mean escapes us.

We use a few words to show willing,
folly in that it misleads our hosts
who ready and hospitable, happily
reply in the argot of their kind,
then we find we do not know, are lost;
it is a test we undergo and always fail,
the oral, so pitiless so friendly,
viva voce in camera that cannot lie.

It appears they learn the language
from an early age and use it all the time,
the dialect of their daily lives,
a discipline and life-long extra,
lingua franca for them world-wide;
but for us, only heard in our great need
and half understood, on special occasions
as sorrow, sickness, grief and tribulations.

Laurie Bates

IV.   These Thy Servants

28. HWYL

In the old days, when giants
were truly giants and preachers
preachers, the dark man
in many a pulpit would step

into the hwyl and hammer
the devil unconscious till Tuesday
with battle-fury of Celtic
heroical eloquence.

Today, it seems that Satan
is given the play's best lines.
The hwyl has died and left
only an ad-man's hype.

Robert Irwin

29. INVICTUS (WELL, NEARLY)

The Reverend Invictus Phillips
believed he might be a fresh
Messiah. When he was young
he had most of the attributes.

Every morning he'd nail
his soul to a cross of self-
denial as huge as a giant
Californian redwood.

He loved his neighbours as much
as he loved himself. He'd preach
his hopeful gospels to any
who had the time to listen.

Eventually he was ordained
as minister – collar and all:
and that's where the rot set in -
he couldn't stand the pace

of deacon's meetings and teas
for chapel roofs, and dead
committees – forever committees
where he had to take the chair.

It wasn't Apollyon
who defeated him – just good folk
with their self-perpetuating
and feather-weight churchiness.

Messiahship was forgotten.
His anchors dragged. At last
he grounded, a derelict lightship
burnt out on a bleak shore.

Robert Irwin

30. NEW BROOM

Our new minister certainly
gets things done. He tells
us all the hard-nosed facts
and economics of worship:

demands the due amount
from each of us. Annual
balance-sheets never looked better
and neither did the chapel.

New carpets now! And pew
cushions on every seat;
and the fragrance of fresh paint
greeting you like incense.

We sing our hymns from new
trendy books; our choir
stands robed in white like a Ku
Klux Klan conventicle.

It wasn't like this when our old
minister was alive.
He didn't seem to care
too much about the cash-flow.

The place was shabbier then,
but somehow homely. No
seeker for love or truth
went away empty.

Robert Irwin

31. CHURCH CONFERENCES

There's some desperate saintliness about the way
good people are turned on by these methodic
meetings in chapels musty with holiness
and Ronuk. A packed agenda is their joy,
their raison d'être. A point of order fills
their cup to overflowing.
      I have seen
decrepit Ministers bounce like budgies when
some juicy piece of controversy bobbed
up into "any other business;" In back seats
we feebler delegates scowled and thought of home.

We'd all been too preoccupied to notice
God slipping out after the opening prayer.

Robert Irwin

32. THE PEWMAN

Look, said the atheist,
you and this god of yours,
this supraterrestrial irresistible force
with a personal point of view
and all that palaver you call the Word -
you really annoy me, you do;
for don't you see,
it's totally, utterly, indisputably
absurd?
       I know, said the Pewman.

Bad enough, said the atheist,
your talk of a Father, but then there's a Son,
and here, god bless us all, there's another one,
sent by the Son - if I've got that right? -
buzzing around in your brain
(no wonder you can't think straight)
as a last resort?
It's all so irrational, so *unlikely* - in short
it's insane.
       I know, said the Pewman

So, then, said the atheist,
we come to that maiden mild
with a child out of wedlock, seemingly the child
of the Father in heaven – a clever ruse
(distance no object, can't fail)
with an earthly father to stand in the Father's shoes.
Well pardon me
if I call that a blether, a blague, a sheer fantasy,
a fairy tale.
       I know, said the Pewman.

Worst, said the atheist,
is your habit of breaking bread
with a vagabond phantom, ages on ages dead,
who comforts, counsels, forgives
for the price of a drop of wine;
but can you say truly, he *lives*?
for the last time,
think, man, why don't you think, it isn't a crime,
just *think!*
    I *know,* said the Pewman.

Walter Nash

33. CHOIRS

The choirs start up
past midnight, smart
men in suit and tie
with bursting red faces
and mouths open like
fish synchronised in a
duplicity of sound that
fills the flapping tent
and rises like flames
to the starlit sky.
Six uncles in the front
row and two at the back –
my father's space now
empty at the side.

A rich blend of voices
that close your eyes, lets
you drift away to places
where only angels sleep.

Idris Caffrey

34. THE LIVELY CHRISTIANS

We are the morning congregation
gathered in goodwill and fellowship here,
for Authorised Version and Holy Communion,
armoured in Faith and our best gear;
some are noble ruins of wars and years,
all are strong towers of praise and prayers.

The men are fewer, and some of them show
their age and like old timepieces,
inclined to wheeze and be a bit slow,
but from the best Maker, with handsome worn faces;
loyal and reliable, our strength and stay,
what loss to the Church if they were away.

Firm and kind and by Time undismayed,
the ladies run the show, they have the power,
like precious watches that were made
by the great Horologist in His finest Hour,
their little jewelled wheels go round and round.
bright and busy as ever, and just as sound.

Some of us troubled in our lives
may count our days with a downcast eye;
how Faith and Hope, and the Spirit revive
in that lively Christian community;
and how like charms of birds in dark winter,
these ladies lift our lives and make them brighter.

Laurie Bates

35. EVENSONG

On entering the waiting cathedral, waves of the
incense-filled notes of the organ lap at our ears;
Then as the serious melodies magnify
soon we submerge in the
flood-tide of harmony.

Under the dark folded panelling
choristers, neat in their pleated milk surplices,
sway in the candlelight.
Voices are stretching and pressing to heaven
till, like foam covered breakers when coming to
shore, they move to a final amen and our
soul-ships sail close to the harbour.

But although not yet fit for an ending,
now we depart from the church
with some portion of peace,
and drift out on the ebb-stream of light.

David Russell

36. CHAPEL ON A WINTER'S NIGHT

The trapped air cools
cut flowers shiver
in their vase of ice –
pews crack,
the Bible moves
on its lectern.

The chapel's pulse
throbs through the night –
a small flake of confetti
tries to free itself
from a cobweb of frost.

Tomorrow I will come
to sit with you,
finding no better place
to say goodbye.

Idris Caffrey

37. THE BENEDICTION

Still, in the polished air
one yard apart
the black shapes kneel.
Each silhouette is a woman,
each black veil, a nun.
Designed as praying machines,
the habit encloses each.
Inside, the sanctuary flame
burns steadily.
Silent years heave by.
Nothing happens.
Everything happens.
Music lilts, petals fall,
rosary beads click and clatter
as the outside light
drifts away,
another Sunday evening
given back to God.

Pat Jourdain

V. Theologies

38. LA CONDITION HUMAINE

Why are we here?
What (on earth) are we supposed to do (or be)?
Is our span of worth (to anyone?) or of nothing to nobody?
Since few bother to maintain our presence is accidental,
The human being not being just another animal
But that driven by overpowering abstract emotion
So immense as to be any cranium's instinctive governor,
The reason for our fact, being here displayed,
We are "here" to become complete – nothing less (or more).
Our breath is of no consequence in itself
But expression of its own subsidiary role;
Only thereby is our inner drive explained
To have us inevitably face our unfaceable
Which we all endeavour somehow to avoid.

A. B. Challen

39. until KingdomCome

until KingdomCome
men will fight over whose God is right –
they will martyr for The Cause
until KingdomCome
and Truth is personally revealed,
they will grip their holy books and cry
"we're the rightful heirs of paradise!"
until KingdomCome
and the Righteous One appears
with glory beyond dumbfounding words
men will bend prayers hoping God knows
they're bedevilled by infidels
until KingdomCome
and God's Son outshines luciferous glow
more effulgent than conflagrant stars
men will say prophetic voices
have made them furiously right
to execrate this earth of godlessness
until KingdomCome
the meek hide in prayer and discretely
move between this world and next
smuggling with them secrets of the light
and answers to the dark, while they watch
and implore the LordofAll Jesus Christ
to split the skies and KingdomCome

Philip Wesley Comfort

40. MARTYRS

God will surely reward
two kinds of martyrs: the wise
folk who could dare a truth
others called heresy -
maintain in the flames' heat
integrity of mind;

and those who simply held
even in the stakes' chains,
whatever faith was taught
in childhood, after the new
supplanting ideas became
orthodoxy's creed.

Robert Irwin

41. SONNET TO A PLAIN CROSS
(at Offa House, Warwickshire)

His cross stands bravely on the gentle lawn,
defying me to probe the shrubs beyond,
or seek to penetrate the curtain torn
through which my soul may find its final Bond.
"They shall not pass beyond this mask of death!"
proclaims this ikon of a dying God.
"They shall not pass until their latest breath,
and then, maybe, they'll see me give the nod."

Till then defiantly it glares at me to say,
"This is the point where ends your little life.
Faith, hope and love are all you have to play
God's game of cat and mouse, of peace and strife."
Yet reassuringly I can give thanks
his wisdom is as thick as those two planks.

Owen Vigeon

[Ed: For those who do not know the expression, "thick as two [short] planks"
is the demotic for "dense", "thick-witted", "stupid". But the Cross is not "thick",
or "dense", or "solid" in the popular meaning. A reference, too, to 1 Corinthians,
where the cross is "sheer folly" and "Christ nailed to the cross... is the wisdom of
God."]

42. A QUESTION

Tall chestnuts lean their branches to the river.
Strong trunks are anchored by the spread
of clinging roots; their palmate leaflets quiver
under their pyramids of white and red,
the whispering voice of water never ceasing.
Deep in the shade are buttercups and grasses,
tremulous when a sudden gust increasing
sets all the branches swaying as it passes.

Where does it come from, this miraculous power
that splits a seed to thrust into the light
a solid chestnut tree, a meadow flower,
new life – or old preserved in ammonite?
The living cells' divisions only show
the more we analyse, the less we know.

Joan Sheridan Smith

43. LOGOS

What you are loses itself
deliberately in translation:
only occasional fey
poets or prophets have glimpsed

inside the hollow hills
of imagination their flawed
visions of secret roots
under the tree of life.

You are a Word hiding
in self-obscuring clues -
the cambium nudging out
the growth-rings of the wood

for every hay-rack and cross
where solid nails pin down
Truth like a butterfly
not fully understood

Robert Irwin

44. GETTING ANSWERS

Sometimes you answer before any chance
even to ask the question and unmask
the need or problem, as unimpeded
as the prophet Isaiah prophesied.
Yet now I am disendowed, repeating
myself like a thesaurus and sighing
as those persistent waves that rant and leave
rippled evidence of their fragile grips.

A.K.Whitehead

45. LOST

Lost
in my King James and black cage
amongst the pages
of this prophesy

Devotion
tied to the chains
of guilt and fear,
this strict discipline
of book and answer.

What calls
beyond the ink
and ages of this legacy?

The lamb
in white simplicity.

I had thought
it was a promise
but now, realise
it is a gauntlet:

and the hardest one of all.

M. Bedford

46. TO SEEK

To seek God is to seek truth,
To find truth is to find Love;
To love Love is to find faith;
To find faith is to find power;
To have power is to share
in the divine nature
and to know the nothingness
of self's infinite value.

A .K .Whitehead

47. FREESTYLE

Freedom means joining the dance,
the grand chain of all the stars,
where everyone knows the step
and everyone's freelance.

Where motion and rest are one
and speed thrills in the cliffs,
where quietness is flight,
and effort is gone.

Susan Glyn

48. REPETITIOUSLY

We run away
into ourselves
attempting to escape
that which never
existed.

We run away
and back again
ever searching
to repeat experiences
with perfection.

We run away
in open secrecy,
one of a multitude
seeking to relive
origin's first day.

Paul Truttman

49. ONLY THE WOUNDED

'By his wounds you have been healed,'
we read.
'Tis thy wounds our healing give,'
we sing.
'Only the wounded can heal,'
it is said.

Again we read
God has appointed those who have
gifts of healing, but
only the wounded can heal,
we are told.

What, then, does this divine appointment
signify –
a gift of wounds?

Pray now for the right and full use
of what has been received,
the mystery of the gift
bestowed.

With thanksgiving.

John L. W. Robinson

50. SPRING THOUGHTS

In the dappled sun-shade of the may
on the edge of the big wood
I am watching the butterflies –
peacock, holly blue, orange tip, speckled wood
dance through the shafts of gold
and the drifting petals.

It would be really hard, I imagine,
to create such deliberate beauty: but then
it took God to think
of making a caterpillar
and then letting it all
just happen.

William Rowell

51. FEATHER

Trodden in the leaf litter,
it is no more than
a relic from an ageing bird.
Then the child stoops,

claims it as her own.
To her, it is the magic quill
that wrote the spell of Autumn:
pearl smooth, translucent.

To her biologist father
it is a moment's aid, evidence
of wing shape and type,
perfection in barb and keratin.

To the bird itself, it is life,
skin, bone, flight, courtship,
pride. And yet it remains
- a feather.

Pauline Kirk

52. BRIGHT SKY

Humming at great height:
well-tuned world ticking over;
or as sun glowed then lit,
celestial generator;
or vibrant resonance
of tomcats in their puissance.

Bright sky dazzled,
light broke in splinters;
swan-silver, shower of gold,
flame of fires;
it is Leviathan
Lord of Upper Air and Heaven.

All-powerful, male, content,
Managing Director of the Universe,
at ease in his proper element
on course for Olympus,
Zeús in his amours protean,
flies in as Boeing 747.

Laurie Bates

53. MRS GOD'S RESPONSE

Theologian
analysing
sentences of doom:
parsing
indefinite article of faith:
cataloguing
the three persons of grammar
and of divinity:
always for him
the masculine
gender has precedence.

One day, perhaps, some poor
heart-broken
Mother will appear
crashing through clouds to drag
her daft son home.

Robert Irwin

54. MIRACLES

Miracles tumble off pegs
in such an assortment of sizes
colours and shapes and styles
that every situation
is guaranteed one to fit.

But miracles seldom appear
precisely as expected:
designs often differ
widely from our proposals
in sudden lovely surprises.

Miracles are sometimes
invisible to our eyes.
we don't know they've happened
till we look deep in the magic
mirror that some call faith.

The miracle of "No"
may often mean God's "Yes,"
that touches hopelessness
and turns it into grace,
and changes "Stop" to "Go".

Robert Irwin

55. SOLACE IN DECEMBER

"I'm always glad when Christmas has
gone by," he had said,
on more than one occasion.

And now I feel the force and meaning
of his words,
spoken long ago.

Waiting, too, in the queue
for stamps, I heard one shopper
say to another
"All you can do is just
be thankful for what has been,
that's all,
you can't do any more."

John L.W.Robinson

56. JUDGEMENT

Repent? Of course I don't!
Because I don't know, yet, why I'm accused.
It's a blank form to fill up for myself.

That's unfair! "Sins I know not of"?
and "Things I left undone"?
Black marks against me that I never knew

when I was doing fine. Or so I thought.
Or did I? Have I ever thought?
        Or even thought I *ought*?

        I'll score myself a nought.

Susan Glyn

57. THE DAY THE CAT LEARNT TO SPEAK
(For Virginia)

The day the cat learnt to speak, she said.
"I will praise the Lord my God for what
I have seen today: People broken
For ages, joining together without glue.
The dead, raised to life, coming
Through the floor to greet me. The
Sly dog and the field mouse leaping through
The open door to sit beside me,
And everyone dancing for the first time.
Clouds blown apart by the wind,
Revealing a new heaven and earth
And time stretching momentarily
Before being puffed out of all existence."

Simon Baldock

58. WHERE YOU ARE
(for Jonathan James, b.May 16th, 1995 – d. May 28th , 1995)

Where you are
the lungs renew themselves
perpetually.

Where you are
the atmosphere is mild enough
for the most delicate skin.

Where you are
the food's good and the service excellent
all the time.

Where you are
spinsters are embraced
and childless uncles
make entertainments for the unborn.

Where you are
the sad are comforted,
the homeless housed.
the hungry fed,
the sick made whole
and the only hands with scars
are the Surgeon's

Nick Ware

VI Comings and Gainrisings

59. A.N.OTHER

At first assumed in streams,
stones, growing things, creatures
that scurry, flitter, dream, devise:

Otherness worshipped in moons'
orbits, suns' spinnings; transposed
from stars to fables: inferred

from a hive's hum: at last
drawn from one nailed Man's grave –
Other affirmed in flesh.

Robert Irwin

60. BORN IN A BARN

Cock-crow, light reddening the eastern sky
a new-born infant's cry –
and in the barn behind the village inn,
a tired young woman rests on bales of straw,
holding a warm damp body wrapped within
her arms. Her husband sweeps the earthen floor,
clears afterbirth and soaking bloody rags.
She watches, half asleep.

News travels fast, and visitors arrive
with morning light. Shepherds are kneeling on the earth.
The child lies sleeping in his manger bed,
wound round with linen, as one day he'll be,
laid in a grotto meant to house the dead –
awaiting his rebirth.

Joan Sheridan Smith

61. ILLEGAL IMMIGRANT

They said you stayed a few
sight-seeing years and went
jet-setting back to the spacey
places where you belonged.

But your passport was never stamped
by any competent
official; authority never
sanctioned your visit here.

You slipped in by the back
door of a stable: out
by the route of a dicey cave
and a wobbly stone unsealed.

Ascension to the clouds
witnessed by just a few
dazed superstitious bumpkins
and a couple of stray angels?

A likely cover story
for a pre-conceived deception!
You were no tourist – no!
You came meaning to stay.

Your sufferings were not
short spasms at Golgotha.
You're rumbled! You still ache
when we ache – groan for groan,

whatever griefs we know
are yours. When some child dies
in Namibia or Neath,
brother, you're dying too.

No dodgy immigrant now -
through suffering you have earned
what weird satisfaction you find
in belonging to our world.

You've paid your taxes of tears
and rejections; your Union dues
of anguish are all marked up:
yes, God, you are one of us!

At last it's beginning to dawn -
you really weren't kidding that time
when you said to your worried few
mates, "I am with you always."

Robert Irwin

62. ΙΧΘΥΣ

ΙΧΘΥΣ was once a sign
on catacombs and martyr's homes
signalling allegiance to the Nazarene.
those who knew him claimed him Christ
and swore – not to Caesar – he was God's Son
the only begotten risen Savior.
Christianoi they called them, humanity's haters,
atheists, Oedipists and Thysteans
secretive, aloof, born of Nazareth's joke
snuffed by Rome for superstition
from Nero to Diocletian they burnt them –
their bodies their bones their books.
Domitian, Trajan, Hadrian purged them
but they refused their noxious incense,
already burning for
ΙΗΣΟΥΣ
ΧΡΙΣΤΟΣ
ΘΕΟΥ
ΥΙΟΣ
ΣΟΤΗΡ
for they'd rather flame than flicker.

Philip Wesley Comfort

[Ed: The Greek letters of the title form a word meaning "fish" (the Latinised version is <u>icthus</u>) The separate letters stand for "Jesus Christ, Son of God, Saviour" – the message spelled out at the end of the poem.]

63. ICHTHUS

Two strangers meet
on the dangerous street. Innocuous
conversation: weather:
the price of food. A toe
doodles a fish-shape in dust;
casually wipes it. The other
repeats the gesture. Ties
of brotherliness are averred.

Ichthus: the small pollan
the sons of Zebedee knew
in Galilee long ago:
the strong salmon fighting
adverse currents to spawn
in quiet pools of peace.

Robert Irwin

64. ALMOST YOU

You almost came into my space today –
so empty now, devoid of shape,
rough-edged and sharp,
hurting.
Just for an instant almost you
but long enough for hope to fly,
the heart to flutter faster than before.
Beyond the wall you pass
then out of reach –
and far away in time, transfixed,
me behind glass.
I saw you walking by
cap at a certain angle
and head bent –
just for a moment you were there,
then went.

Josie Davies

65 READING THE HEAVIES

The poet filched his verses, so we hear;
the hero ran away, the prophet lied;
this guardian of the law abetted crimes,
that spoiler of the poor was sanctified.
The evidence? The broadsheets make it clear –
read all about it in *The Sunday Times*.

We like to see the pickaxe put to use,
the lofty reputation hacked away;
our anxious interest in the good and great
is to exonerate our feet of clay,
their being only human our excuse
for being irredeemably third rate.

So, what if Jesus, in awakened power,
His majesty ablaze, should come again,
ready to reassume the flesh and scale
a new Golgotha, and re-live His pain –
how would we read the story of that hour?
How would the Sunday papers tell the tale?

Week One: "Christ on the Cross – we name and shame
the Perpetrators of the Dreadful Act."
Week Two: "Was it a Fake? A Doubt exists –
We separate the Fable from the Fact".
Week Three: "Analysis of 'Saviour's' Claim –
'No Afterlife', say Government Scientists."

Walter Nash

66. A SECOND COMING

I saw Jesus again today. He drove up in
the new silver Mercedes, dressed
in that pin-striped Brooks Brothers suit,
sitting next to J.I.,
the head of p.r. for our firm.

I felt we'd set him up right.
The only thing wrong
was the hair and the beard. I waited till
we'd had a few Scotch and Perriers
till I mentioned my reservations.
Flower children. Peace. Those
went out in the Sixties. Slightly
unshaven, maybe – but not a full bush.

He said he would have to think about it,
so I know he'll give in, much as he has
with everything else. I mean,
who'd listen to him the way he was,
in that crazy cloak and flip-flops?
He'll get so much better coverage now,
with the Last Supper live by satellite
from Maxim's, and a stunt man doing
the Crucifixion bit, with an extra or two
for the Tomb scene, though we've taken out
a huge policy, just in case some sick
publicity hound decides to do him in personally.

All of this, a second time around,
he objected violently to at first,
but when he saw that we were right,
that no one would ever believe it *at all*
if he didn't let us handle it *our* way,
then he waxed philosophical about it –
got even a little indifferent – which made
the rest of us panic a little,
thinking he might not go through with it.
I mean, he seems so passive, so apathetic,
so now we're just trying to humour him along –
trying to make him see reason.
We're quite willing to negotiate.
He can't have given up on us.
We've certainly not given up on *him*.

William Ruleman.

67. ALTERNATIVE PORTRAIT

Holman Hunt painted
a lanterned and thorn-scarred Christ
outside a bolted door
meekly seeking admission.

Another with such skill
might show an opposite concept -
a grey, desperate God
in Everyman's spidery cupboard
hammering for release.

Robert Irwin

68. TIME PLAN

He will come again
But it is as well to recognise that
So many light years had to pass
Before the blazing death of a star
Mimicking His on earth
Would reach out to us
To bathe us in its light
And lead us to a manger
And that the light of His Death
Exploding on our earth
May yet fade to darkness
So that somewhere in a dusting of stars
The final shining of our own star
Long after it becomes a cinder
May lead others onward
To where a miracle is born.

Richard Unwin

VII Mythologies

69. EVE THE GARDENER

Eve was bored with her paradise garden.
Everything was planned when she came to it.
Her wishes hadn't been consulted.

She would have liked a pergola,
A small rock garden and a shrubbery,
the tallest sunflowers, pompom dahlias,
runner beans and a herb garden.
And little tasks: seeds to sow and water,
bulbs to lift, even deadheading
(because, being the Lord's, all the flowers
were in bud or full bloom, obstinately fresh).
She said to Adam, "Do what you want today.
I shall be in the orchard."

The rest is mythic history

Now Adam has long since served his sentence
of toil among the thorns and thistles.
He works at a desk instead; the bread he eats
sits ready sliced on supermarket shelves.
But Eve still humbly kneels, wrestling with the soil;

fights weeds, hunts down slug and snail,
greenfly and mildew, despairs in the drought,
sweeps autumn leaves, finds earwigs in the roses.
Such is her punishment for talking to the snake.

But sometimes she'll stand and look over her Eden plot,
her hands in gardening gloves with shears or secateurs,
a trug on the ground beside her, full of greenery,
and smile, because the good and generous Lord
has let her make a garden for herself.

Isabella Strachan

70. RAHAB REGRETS

A scarlet thread should bind, not separate.
'Rahab'. they said, *'bring out the spies who came.*
The times are dangerous, and it is late'.

'The men had gone before the city gate
was shut', I lied. A harlot has no shame.
(But scarlet threads should bind, not separate.)

I hid them where the stalks of flax lie straight –
the roof. *'Israelites,'* I said to them,
'the times are dangerous, and it is late.

fear patters like the rats about our state.
I've saved your lives. Swear that you'll do the same'.
(A scarlet thread should bind, not separate.)

'Our lives for yours' they said. With rope, I let
them down. *'Tie this scarlet thread to the frame*
when times are dangerous and it is late,

we'll know to spare your house'. I took the bait,
uneasy fish playing the line for time –
a scarlet thread should bind, not separate –

and tied it when the soldiers marched in sight.
Our city walls collapsed, and Joshua's aim –
for times were dangerous and it was late –

achieved: our treasures seized, my neighbours meat
for vultures, me and mine in an alien home.
A scarlet thread should bind, not separate,

and I, who lied, and hid the spies, regret.
Predestined? I am still to blame,
a scarlet thread should bind not separate
but times are dangerous and it is late.

Pat Buik

[Ed: The story of Rahab, the prostitute of Jericho, who hid Joshua's spies, and was
spared after the fall of the city, is told in the book of Joshua, chaps. 2 and 6]

71. BATHSHEBA'S MAID

He was a kind man, my master:
I wept when he was killed. She did, as well.
Shut herself up and spoke to nobody.
Guilty, of course. I can't say anything.
If it had been me the King sent for
I think I would have gone. So handsome!
The king, I mean. Not gentle like her husband.
Strong, cruel they said at times.
She was powerless to resist. Her belly
is swelling with his child. He'll marry her,
everyone knows how it was done.
If I were to attempt
to kill *my* man, as sometimes I've dreamed
after a night of violent abuse,
what would become of me? Uriah cared.
For all his lovely wife he'd time for me.
Not in a shameful way, you understand,
but kind. He warned my cruel man.
Not that it did much good. To be quite fair,
she often took me in her arms,
a loving mistress. What shall I do now?
Will she take me to David's palace too?

Joan Sheridan Smith

72. THE MAGI

Probably Zoroastrian priests,
they came in we don't know what number
climbing over the Zogros mountains
out of decadent, lovely Persia
with its fountains and gardens
and over-sophistication.
When they, at last, found the baby
now a toddler, in the barbarous land,
having been given so much,
might they not have been given so much more –
as they gave Him gold, frankincense, and myrrh –
and then headed back,
avoiding Herod's palace,
unaware of the slaughter they caused,
without the daytime cloud
or night-time star,
as they plodded back
over the monotonous path,
while drinking the mind-releasing haoma,
some vision of the cross
in terms of light and dark,
fire and water,
as they nodded on their camels
over the dry rocks
and parched mountain passes?

Bill West

[Ed: haoma, in Persian mythology a sacred plant, whose sap had anaesthetic qualities and was drunk during sacrifices. Haoma was defined by Zarathustra (Zoroaster) as the power that renews life, but in spiritual terms. It is similar to the Vedic soma]

73. ALSO ABOUT THAT TIME

Beside the shore of Galilee
was also born about that time
Peter the Rock, as he came to be;
and all his faithful life laid down,
until at last he was carried from
his cell in Rome to martyrdom.

Not far away and about then,
the girl was born near Galilee
we know as Mary Magdalen;
by what strange paths came she to be
first in the garden, grievingly:
'Noli me tangere'

And also in a loving home
not too far from Galilee
proudly they gave their son his name;
nor ever dreamed that it would be
a brand to burn them cruelly,
the synonym for treachery.

Laurie Bates

74. A SHEPHERD'S TALE

I mind well, though many years have passed.
We'd seen the star that shone all week
go overhead and Ezra, the watch
along o' me, pointed his staff
to trace its fire, a jewel among chaff
so feeble glimmered other stars, hotch-potch
of glows against that brilliant streak
of light which slashed the night in two.
Doctor, it frightened us, I tell you straight,
followed us round the sheep
till we met our pals fast asleep
inside their cloaks, lead weight
fatigue upon their eyes; ours, too,
as we talked to keep awake, to fight
the weariness that lambing brings.
You're always on the go, what with
wolves and wind, and frost with teeth
like daggers: and filthy sleet which stings
like whips when you're on the heights. . .
you know it, too. Well, we got back
safe and hugged the fire, when Ezra says
"What's that yonder, coming close?
That star again?" An' we froze
in fear, bathed in a golden haze
before we flung ourselves upon the track,
hiding our faces like the rest. They'd woken
scared to death by the burning cloud,
for something. . . someone had appeared and stood
before us, calming us. I peeped from my hood
and saw an angel telling about
what God, Almighty God, had spoken.
Good news, he said, great joy
for everyone, in Bethlehem born
that very night, the Deliverer, our Messiah,
our Jewish Lord. I gazed higher
and saw so many angels, like dawn
lighting the east, filling the sky

and singing music I can't describe –
but I'll remember to my dying day
their words: "Glory to God in the highest
heaven, and to men on earth He rests
His favour, peace!" Then ray on ray
of light bounced all around to inscribe
the night with gold. Doctor, we were afraid
no more, but listened and watched amazed,
scarce believing what we saw an' heard.
Stranger still, the sheep never stirred,
but chewed the cud content or grazed,
their warm breath freezing on the blade,
and frost riming their backs, so cold
it was; yet the light about them hot
an'the singing warming us to the core.
Then the angel spoke once more.
"Look for this sign," he said. "Not
far from the lodging-house is an old
stable. You'll find the baby there,
in a manger, wrapped in swaddling clothes.
He is the Messiah, the Holy One."
An', doctor, scarcely had he done
when the light began to fade. Loath
to leave that place, all we did was stare
at where the angels disappeared, a cloud
of light which shrank to a pin-point
in the sky, till cold and sleet brought
us back to earth. We made short
work of the mileage into town, joined
others in the stable-crowd,
for all was as the angel said. A child
was there, his mother with Joseph Barjacob
from Nazareth of Judah's tribe.
But what's all this to you, a Gentile scribe,
a Greek? I'm keeping you from your job
letting my tongue run wild.
What can this mystery mean, young Doctor Luke?

John Waddington-Feather

75. MARTHA'S CONVERSION

Often, as they sit,
someone has to make the tea
and the washing must be done today.
Today.
I know the feel of water and raw meat,
the coils of peel, the scouring-out of pans.
These textures teach me nothing now.
As a grain of rice in the salt,
sliver of orange in the tea,
yeast rising in the dough,
so his ideas run through me.

Yet there is no time
and Magdalene
has always escaped
into that free land where he is.
She becomes even younger,
forcing me into a mother-shape of caring.

Tomorrow perhaps I shall sit
with Lazarus in the sun, let go
these elaborate details
and talk out our mystery.

Pat Jourdain

76. LAZARUS SPEAKS

after Lazarus was raised
he said nothing we know of
he didn't write a book
or go on tour
he just sat there
        he didn't speak
of paradise or hades
and didn't say
if he was glad
to be back
        Mary and Martha thrilled
and so did Jerusalem
but the leaders
wanted him stilled as a tomb
in case he had a story

Philip Wesley Comfort

77. THE EXECUTION

And being tired, they brought their horses
to the evening stream to drink.
The sunset crimsoned everything,
but bloodier still it gleamed when one
washed clean his spear,
and they who'd nailed the trio
to their crosses washed their armour
of the gore that clung all day.
As darkness fell they'd had to finish off
the two who lasted out,
and wipe away much stinking blood and sweat.
The ending of the third was somewhat cleaner:
one spear-thrust doubly-sured
the death his flogging wrought.
He hung already dead,
stripped of the robe the king himself had given –
a joke-cloak for his bleeding back
to match his vicious crown
the jailers set upon his head.

Odd that he died the instant
that the tremor shook the ground and hushed the baying crowd.
The horses' chilling screams
and grating armour of the cavalry
closing ranks, half expecting
something worse, cluttered the silence.
For such a stillness fell,
so awesome and oppressive,
like lull before a storm that never broke,
and only frightened murmurs from the mob
rippled the gallows' foot.

Daylight's ebb dispersed them all
to make their paschal sacrifice,
satisfied they'd seen the couple
finished off who'd hung there cursing.
The one already dead
was handed to his friends;
highly illegal, of course,
but that's the way it goes
when rank is squared.

All done, the cavalry brought
their horses to the stream to drink.
leaving the blood-soaked crosses
to the night.
Time enough to fell them
once the Passover had passed;
but light was sour, dying, and they had still
to make the sacrifice at camp
to appease their vengeful gods.

John Waddington-Feather

78. JUDAS

He betrayed me, you know;
history is a liar if it says otherwise.
When I put my hand in that dish
and his eyes met my eyes,
I knew his wish;
the steady unblinking gaze that ordered: "Go!

Do it now." I knew what I must do,
I, the accomplice chosen to prepare
his triumph, would then tell the Pharisees,
and they would come for him, and there
they'd know his power; down on their knees
salute Messiah revealed, the one, the true.

Why didn't that happen? Why
didn't the glory strike when I kissed his cheek?
Why were they not kneeling, the fools?
I saw then, he was weak,
or beaten. He threw the game. The rules
of play said, then the man must die.

The money? You say my "fee".
Yes, that was a piece of our plot,
a yarn to spin for the clergy's benefit;
but motive? It was not
a question of cash. Nothing to do with it.
I was betrayed. I. *He* betrayed *me.*

Walter Nash

79. THE GOVERNOR'S WIFE

Now at last the afternoon is silent.
The sentence given, the man taken away,
The people gone to celebrate their feast
Of Passover; it marks a time, they say,
When with their faceless God, long years ago,
They brought down plagues upon the land of Pharaoh.
This place is full of tales. Now I can rest,
Although I think the man was innocent.

My husband said he had to give assent
To the man's death, and that his hands are clean
Of blood; that he attempted a release,
And it was his affair. What did I mean?
To execute a man is man's business,
And a woman's to ask for gentleness,
For nothing more than her own inward peace.
Yet I do think the man was innocent.

I lately heard the sound of merriment
Following a donkey through the city.
That was an entry for a king! to go
With trodden branches and hosanna cry.
But why should Romans care? A carpenter
A threat to Caesar? Tell me another!
Even a woman can see through that. So
I still believe the man was innocent.

He's drinking wine with friends now, well content
At trouble over, able to take breath.
My head is aching, and I hope this night
May pass more easily. A nasty death –
But not women's business, except for those
Who see it carried out. How dark it grows!
So much the better, blotting out the sight
Of that good man I know was innocent.

Isabella Strachan

80. HIS FACE

Years afterwards, two men
who'd known him in Nazareth then moved away
met in Jerusalem.
Because the old recall their past, they talked of him.
A Greek who, with Parthians, Medes and Elamites
was visiting the city, joined the two old men,
curious to know what it was
could make them talk so earnestly.
Soon he broke in.

"Yes, I have heard of that philosopher!
In Corinth, Ephesus and Thessalonika
they hold his mystery with bread and wine.
And you knew him? What was he like?"

"We knew him only as a fellow townsman.
Saw him at festivals, at wedding feasts,
or in the synagogue. No more than that."

"How did he look?"

"He had a good face.
An honest face, with eyes that looked at you
as though he saw into your soul,
but passed no judgement on what he saw."

"Joseph, you exaggerate.
I saw nothing unusual in his look.
Nothing to know again."

"Perhaps if one described him with exactitude,
his colouring, his smile, his eyes,
and a Greek who believed in him
set down the likeness faithfully – "

"What then?
It would be but the likeness of a young man's face.
Your world is full of such."

"It would be prized above all the statues seen
in Athens, Alexandria or in Rome."

"You Greeks always know best."

Isabella Strachan

VIII Images and Words

81. ANNUNCIATIONS

Botticelli's angel
has just alighted, and the gentle virgin
sways in the rush and rustle of his wings.
But Donatello's virgin
has risen in surprise to hear the message
(picked out in gold the wall behind her chair)
The best of all is Fra Angelico:
     Such simple line and colour!
     In an arcaded cloister
     the angel bows, his rainbow wings uplifted.
     She sits attentive with hands crossed in prayer
     or mirroring Gabriel, in anticipation
     of cradling. Both are listening.
     Time suspended
     they stay, their heads inclined in reverence.
     This is the moment of the Incarnation.

Joan Sheridan Smith

82. ART OR ARTIST

On loan from the National Gallery
some twenty Flemish paintings, among them
a small Rembrandt nativity, a cool
Vermeer, and a townscape you admired:
a square in Antwerp. But for men in tall black hats
and knee-breeches, much as it is today -
or so you thought. What caught my eye
was altogether different. A large canvas
crowded with figures; 'Christ blessing the Children'
Familiar subject, open to the charge
of sentimental déjà vu. Not so.
This Christ, who sits among fat burghers' wives
in coifs and heavy skirts, is broad and solid,
bare peasant feet spread firmly on the earth.
One strong square hand rests lightly on the head
of a small girl, who's turned away from him,
bored, looking for her mother, or the doll
that she was playing with. She holds a slate.
People crowd round, heads craning, one man hoisting up
a child who sits goggling on his shoulder.
You can almost see them pushing. Christ alone
sits still, his eyes upon this child.
A thoughtful, tender gaze, perhaps because
sooner or later innocence is betrayed.
So taken was I by the painting
that I forgot to note the artist's name.

Joan Sheridan Smith

83. MICHELANGELO'S PIETA

His vision a hunger,
his hands, an urgent clock,
strike blank stone.
Dream voices guide him,
bless his cramped fingers,
his crown of glistening sweat,
A blizzard of dust and jagged rock
fills the air.
He pounds and shatters
until the stone breathes,
releases a mother
who knows nothing of angels or of grace,
feels only the dead weight of her child.

She hears voices calling him *Messiah*
but his blood clings to her like skin.
Liquid salt stings her eyes.
She does not know of faith
or the artist who, like her son,
will give resurrection to this death,
prove that stone can obey,
that sometimes
even God
needs a resting place

Shayla Hawkins

84. MOSES

A multi-nation of tourists fills the chapel,
jostling to collect the Michelangelo Moses,
to add to Tower Bridge, Disney World.

So many years of chiselling, arguing with a Pope,
labouring to release spirit from stone,
and all for tourists to photograph.

Satisfied at last, the crowds leave,
to search for coloured cards and coaches.
For a few shaded minutes, the church is silent.

Before me, marble skin begins to breathe,
folds of neck take on life.
A furious Moses grieves over Israel.

Pauline Kirk

85. THE ABBEY

What was it like in those days?
White walls and painted saints
Glowing with new colours,
The arches' toothed edge
Binding the prayers and incense
Into the plaster,
Into the stone.

The long nave
Too far in the smoky air
To show the sanctuary
Clearly.
Only the flooding aureoles
Bloom golden
On beeswax stems;
Thick as a man's arm,
White as a woman's thigh.
The shrine
Comforting as her body
Familiar as her bed
Canopied for the night.

Richard Maslen

86 FIGURE IN A LANDSCAPE

Often I envy those who by their deft
weavings of shutter speeds and apertures
produce a perfect photograph of God
posed with a fatherly air beneath the tree
of life – with every detail clear and sharp,
sunlight and shade in perfect symmetry.

My effort's like a water-colour, ruined
where rain or teardrops made the washes run
to unintended blendings, or where winds
shook the frail easel. So my view at last
is never more definable than some
amorphous figure in a universe
the colour of a January day.

Robert Irwin

87. FROM AN OLD MANUSCRIPT

Twilight casement,
blue panes and
firelight glow
upon an old picture.
A girl's head
and the poet's fancy
in the stillness.

Music – and
a song remembered
of another scene –
colours – gold ,
white, black and
silver.

Two figures –
the shadowed light,
his song of consolation,
Mozart – and
a beauty beyond
all grief.

Remembered,
heard in dreams.
The singer and the song
through decades lost and gone.

The poet sleeping,
the fire down,
the room dark.

John.L. W. Robinson

88. CAEDMON

It was below the darkness and behind the night,
  More ancient than either; and a sudden spark
  Burnt like a meteor through the flawless dark.
A single shiver ran from abyss to height.

And the dark tore, as though a blade went shearing,
  For those pits of deathly blackness were so thin
  They could rip to show the living darkness within;
They only veiled the shining dark of beginning.

And the joy broke, the vision came with power.
  The frozen sky unfolded into arches,
  where the trees of heaven sent their shimmering branches
he saw the angel of creation rise in fire;

And within him too the song-maker's passion mounted.
  His voice was borne on the cry that both upheld it
  And even into its own mighty utterance bound it;
he could not help but sing. This was commanded.

So tongue-tied Caedmon shared in that summoning,
  The naming of the light before it broke
  Through the waiting forest, and awoke
The worlds that lay asleep in God's foreknowing.

Surely he saw it, surely even now it was coming!
  The brightness, the truth! All mysteries unfolded!
  Even as he strained, the song, the forest, faded.
The night was closing, and only the frost remaining,

Yet he knew he had sung, and knew another had stood here.
  The oxen's sides were trembling, their nostrils dilated;
  The very silence there had been visited;
The presence was not gone from the pricking air.

And next he knew that neither had the singing ceased.
  The quiet night had become its antiphon,
  Containing, echoing it, and for Caedmon
This was his part, the quiet and the beasts.

The song of power was cleaving through the terrors
  He saw the waters of the night divide,
  The wars, the wolves, the sorcery, swept aside,
The ache of iron was healed from a thousand winters.

A frozen midnight and a dream that did not pass.
  He lay in great peace in the straw, and heard,
  still sounding on, the all-creating word;
Above the doorway marched the circling stars,

Turning on the unseen point, on the unheard cry;
  As his own life had rested all along
  On that which he now knew as awakening song;
Beneath his time he had felt it timelessly lie.

And the recognition, the knowing, were everything.
  But then the dreaming cattle stamped and shivered
  As though one passed outside; and he remembered,
Seeming to hear it again, "Caedmon, you must sing."

"And I can sing!" he heard his own glad voice.
  And the words, the beauty came. He sang the Creation
  That had not ceased, and the stars' exultation
Moving for ever; and he watched them rejoice,

Flaring in answer; the harmony was whole.
  But then, with a dream's power to turn about,
  And with a dream's insistence, came the doubt;
The blessed harmony shattered from pole to pole.

"Surely this is also a dream! I am asleep!
  I shall know I am awake when the music has gone."
  Then, like a child, grief-stricken, Caedmon
Fell on the ox's flank and began to weep.

In the first pale colour of the day,
  Osgar the monk came to Caedmon for the milking.
  Always they did this together without talking,
  but Caedmon was full of pain, and heard himself say,

As though to ease it, "Brother, I have so strangely slept.
  I thought I could sing, and woke to find it true.
  But was I not even then dreaming? What think you?"
The other looked at him. And then the song leapt.

Caroline Glyn

[Ed: Caedmon's story, on which Caroline's poem imaginatively builds, is told by
Bede in his *Ecclesiastical History of the English People,* Bk.IV, xxiv]

89. HOLD THAT WORD

Hold that word
That almost escaped,
Pursue the echo.

Hold that place
Where words have failed
On the tip of your tongue.

Hold that thought
Of almost inspiration
Where emptiness intrudes.

Hold that poem
At the moment of waking
Before the white-wash of day.

Hold that prayer
Suspended over the world
And feel Him speak.

Christopher Payne

90. WINTER SCENE

And then he makes the snow.
First, one frail flake, fashioned to perfect shape.
God sees that it is good, makes more and more –
myriads of flakes, scattered on field and tree,
on human habitations, foxholes and forms of hare,
till all is white and clean
and shaped to roundness by the wintry air.
Here are man's footprints, there the birds have been,
and still the quiet snow falls everywhere.

Wilfred Burne

91. KEEPING TIME

As one grows older, puffing past one's prime,
The music seems to miss a beat or two.
There is an art one learns to keep in time.

The hills are higher. The desire to climb
Has vanished even with the promised view
As one grows older, puffing past one's prime.

And one may spend a morning with a rhyme
That will not partner where you want it to.
There is an art one learns to keep in time.

One gives up listening for the grand sublime –
A light toccata or a waltz will do
As one grows older, puffing past one's prime.

Grandfather clocks are those which loudly chime,
Warning the last account is almost due.
There is an art one learns to keep in time.

The orchestra provides the paradigm.
Watch the conductor. Listen for your cue.
As one grows older, puffing past one's prime,
There is an art one learns to keep in time.

Joan Fry

92. STREET PLAYERS

An afternoon of street players –
it really doesn't matter where.
I watch jugglers, acrobats,
Morris dancers, a man on fire.

This is who we are –
our best side out there
amongst the dust of the street
trying to amaze, make each other laugh.

Who is watching but the crowd?
Maybe another unseen who claps silently
but knows the show will never last.

Idris Caffrey

93. THE OLD ARTIST'S PRAYER

Welcome, November. Welcome, the month of the dead.
Welcome, early dusk and crawling cold,
The brown decay of October's torrents of gold;
Now my dead are rising, and I am visited.
There is no life for them but what I give:
Old memories, loves, paintings: why, let them live,
Even if for a little I must die instead.

There are so many of them, to be loved and fed
By my old aching body and aching heart.
And, Lord God, are you with them, do you take that part?
The Living God, and do you come with the dead?
You are doing as always, taking place with the last,
The ruined and forgotten, the wreckage of the past.
Come then, you shall be with them in my own cold bed.

I'm painting for them and for you now, ambers and red,
But my life, my sinews and mind, you are taking indeed,
The colours of comfort, that you pretend to need,
So that strength and death together through my body spread
For though you are humble, though you have truly died,
Your blaze of fire and life cannot wholly hide.
The beating of risen blood is in my head.

Welcome, November and the murk. Welcome, I said.
What do I care for blurred and smarting eyes
If I can give shelter to the dead when they rise,
And if another asks it, too, the living and blessed?
He has filled it all with himself, the rain, the cold,
There is more life than I can see or hold.
And through my hand his flames and amber are shed.

Caroline Glyn

94. ST. MARK

Blood and fire on the night horizon
A smell of death in the streets by day;
Silence in the city of hills and temples
And a young voice shouting far away.

Omens in the returning of the black birds,
Omens on the hearth and in the entrails,
Omens at altars, omens on Caesar's threshold
And in the flying dust of a young man's sandals.

Running alone through the darkening empire,
Shouting into the watching silence,
Scattering the sand of the firelit streets
In the burning spray of divine impatience.

While beside him, swept in another glory,
Bounds the lion, pushing back the sky
Of threat with those towering wings and a seraph's ardour
And the fierce gladness of a young man's eye.

In the same ecstasy of passion and warning
And the same adoration, there they run –
The creature of apocalypse and the young man
Breathless, hoarse, under a bloody sun.

Caroline Glyn

IX Christian Occasions

95. THE ANNUNCIATION

While she was being quiet,
first she smelled a wonderful smell,
better than any apple or any fruit,
better than any blossom or flower,
better than honey or anything cooking:
and then she saw a light –
just a glimmer in the corner,
but it spread and became a special gold
unlike any other golden colour
all over the floor;
And then she heard the question,
which she could yet refuse
but never in the world would.
How could she become the mother of God?
And then she simply said
her soul magnified the Lord,
although what that meant
or how it could even be,
the young woman didn't know;
and then a light unlike the other light
settled on her patient lap,
and she received
the Holy Seed.

Bill West

96. ADVENT

Now come, O God!
The world is drifting,
Its values shifting
And all at sea.

Now come, O God!
We need a shepherd,
And life is peppered
With vanity.

Now come, O God!
Our hearts are aching,
No comfort taking
Materially.

Now come, O God!
Commitment's shallow,
The soul lies fallow
For seed from Thee.

Now come, O God!
Man's hunger turning,
Fulfil his yearning,
Of life the key.

Now come, O God!
Unlock our tensions
And apprehensions
And set us free!

Anne Sanderson

97. OLD MAN IN ADVENT

Old man in Advent, watch the weeks go past,
count the moon down, sense how the tides are making;
feel, in the fall of sleep, or thrust of waking,
your heart's appalling lurch towards its last
beating and breaking.

Calendar, cards, red candles on the sill -
despite your paper flesh and falling sinew,
keep the old rituals; there's a child within you
pleading for hope, a young Redeemer still
willing to win you.

Remembering life, remembering many days
endured in fretted patience, like an illness,
turn from that trouble, give your heart to stillness,
bring mind home from its traffickings, its ways
consumed in shrillness.

The world is strident with the noise of hate.
Fold headlines down, switch off the set, perceiving
the sempiternal din of guns and grieving.
Our souls are almost dead; then mark the date
and pray, believing

somewhere, somehow, beyond the printed strife,
the screened confusions, in a darkness lying,
bedded in straw, in some foul shippon lying,
something is born to bring your soul to life,
and ease your dying.

Walter Nash

98. CHRISTMAS SONG

There are brown tyre-treads in the virgin snow
and your skin turns blue in the cold wind's blow,
and you ain't got nowhere else to go,
and you're on you own on these streets, Lady,
you're on your own down here.

There's no shepherds in these parts, my dear,
no herald angels singing clear,
and the wise men stay at home for a warm and a beer,
and you're on your own on these streets, lady,
you're on your own down here.

The sky is black and there ain't no stars,
and the only lights are the cruising cars
and the neon signs of the downbeat bars,
and you're on your own on these streets, lady,
you're on your own down here.

Yet I heard of a night in a time of old
when the velvet sky turned burnished gold,
as the songs were sung and the tidings told
with the earth and heaven in a single fold,
and they called those streets salvation, lady,
the place was Bethlehem.

William Rowell

99. OH, AT BETHLEHEM!

"Christ is born!"
the rooster crowed one morn,
"Oh, cockadoodle doo!
Christus natus est!

"Quack? Oh, quack?"
quacked the duck.
"When? Oh, when?
Quando? Quando?"

"Last night, last night!"
the black raven cried
"In hac nocte!"

"Where? Oh, where?"
the oxen mooed
"Ubi? Ubi?"

"Baa! Oh, baa!"
replied the sheep, who'd been
with the shepherds, there and then.
"Be- Be- Bethlehem! Oh, at Bethlehem!"

Bill West

100. CHRISTMAS DAY

The field, a still cold glitter,
A thousand frosted spiders' webs
Tinselled the trees.
Mistletoe and holly berries;
Shimmering glass baubles.
A Child is born.

A fox crept from the farmyard,
Chicken feathers in his teeth.
Blessed Life-Giver
Icicles dropped from the hedge,
Tinkling wind-blown chime
In a carillon
Alleluia.
Then shafts of sunlight pierced the sleet.
Now and forever.

P. Lucas

101. CHRISTMAS BABY TALK

Ah, isn't he wonderful?
Look at him,
He's so adorable
Just like his Father

Strong sense of presence
His eyes follow you round,
Full of love
Just like his Father.

That smile
Melts the heart,
Draws everyone to him –
Just like his Father.

Such a shame
He'll grow up to be rejected,
Irrelevant to most –
Just like his Father.

Sharon Morgan

102. SONNET: NATIVITY SCENE

And now at last the everlasting Word
Visits his handiwork, explores his art;
All-powerful King, yet he the part prefers
Of servant mild and poor, to win the heart
Of crude and banished mankind. He his round,
Capacious, spinning miracle now greets,
Whilst dark skies sing and shepherds stand around
With beasts. Creator and creation meet.

Augustus reigns! Already two thirds run,
Man's history is a restless little tale;
The hand that writes it puts aside his pen
For plane and saw, finally, sharp nails,
And, in the drama of the fallen soul,
The playwright now assumes the leading role.

Ronald Parr

103. NATIVITY PLAY

"A Christmas play! Let's write our own!" they said,
so down they sat to work: and work they did.
Many blots later, when the job was done,
they published it triumphantly. But soon
the Censor struck. (A very proper lady,
wife of an Elder, pillar of the church.)
"Children, what's this you've written in Scene Two,
where, after the long trek to Bethlehem,
Joseph remarks 'My feet are killing me'
and further on, the keeper of the inn
says, 'You can use my stable, but it's *smelly'*
my dears, you surely know they didn't talk
like that in Bible times!"

                        And so the play
was finally produced – a chastened cast
of small bored angels, shepherds and wise men
mouthing the old familiar seventeenth
century script (all pirated of course,
straight from the King James Version.) It fell flat.

God grant us wisdom from the mouths of babes,
that we may see the sweat-and-bunion true
Nativity that walks our roads each day.

Robert Irwin

104. JOSEPH THE CARPENTER

My dreamy-eyed ancestral
namesake never knew
dreams half as bright as mine.

His sheaves and stars were dull,
commonplace, beside
my splendid angels, who spoke

such splendid mysteries
of a son, who was the Son
of Yahweh's sacred spirit.

And all those trips they planned!
To Egypt: Israel:
and back to Nazareth!

No wonder the donkey's tired
and old before his time -
he's not the only one!

I've seen that boy's bar-mitzvah,
and marvelled at the strange
dreamings behind *his* eyes.

My job's done now. I'll lay
my chisels down in peace,
and dream a quiet death.

Robert Irwin

105. THE STORY

Snow I can believe:
when the wind flew down from Kazakhstan
Bethlehem bowed its head beneath the hills,
the white flood seeped under the stable door
and wise men from that day to this
have always tracked the brightest star
and shepherds...well... what do you think
this upland limestone's for but sheep?
Angels? Yes, granted they're a threatened breed
even where mesas and sierras range.

Of course I don't deny
the recurrence of those homeless
who walk streets to fill in forms -
those families kindly thought
less than 'normal' in some way.
Well, quite, he wasn't the baby's father
and she had some woman's tale to tell...

No, I can take all that:
none of it's any odder than
the sort of thing you hear of now
in Bogota, Sarajevo or Huddersfield
after a drink when the bars close
or in a flat with curtains drawn.
It's just that - well, they thought it mattered so,
mattered enough to tell, for all the world as if

the insignificant were significant,
a local life the greatest story
and bearded God applauding his own play
as all conjoined to write the script
excepting that baby whose lines came later,
who found death in the way of life
and walked to it
and went through it
and rose from it,

quite certainly becoming – human

Ken Smith

106. WELCOME THE CHILD SHE BEARS

Welcome the child she bears,
sweet as the sunset and the starry sky,
chill in the windrush and the silent snow
angel whispers drifting by.

A child to walk alone,
caught in the updraught of an eagle's wings,
sharp as the sandfall in the turning glass,
lost in the song she sings.

A child of different worlds,
touched by silver of a madcap moon,
framed in the frostwork of the winter trees,
learning to die too soon.

William Rowell

107. EPIPHANYTIDE

In time of war
they all set out
with gifts of gold,
the gold of youth.

Some gave their all,
did not return,
one was shot down,
another died
and others lost unknown.

Such golden worth,
all gold unpriced,
a value never guessed,
given and lost
in parting clouds,
an offering and a quest.

Still for the old
a setting out,
a seeking still,
no more with gold.

Only an ascending prayer,
the frankincense of after years
and still attendant myrrh.

John L. W. Robinson

108. CANDLEMAS

February winds bend naked trees
in days of sleet or heavy rain,
and coughs and colds resound indoors.
But night contracts with evening's blue
and snowdrops pearl the garden beds.
Though Eastertide has not yet dawned,
a light shows palely through the gloom
for those with whom the Church's year
keeps track with quiet, unforced pace.
It's Candlemas; the epilogue
to angels and Epiphany.
Two country people, with their gifts
of turtledoves in Temple, heard
Anna and Simeon, who saw,
beyond the old Mosaic law
and dandled infant, that the sun
had risen over Israel,
to shine upon the Gentiles' world.

Isabella Strachan

109. I SURRENDER

to the way Spring sunlight catches me unawares
slanting into the room,
sneaking under tables and chairs,
making the dull grey floor turn bright,
overpowering its down-trodden cussedness;
in league with the window in its revolt
against being so long unnoticed
by covering it in gold-dust.

I hadn't felt any seasonable urge
to force me to spring-clean,
but now it's a *must*.
I was cocooned in the cosiness of cold.
But Winter can't win.
Now I surrender to the Spring's upsurge.
Though I may double-lock the door, and draw the bolt,
Easter will sweep its way in.

Susan Glyn

110. IN EASTER SEASON

Against grey and umber thickets of branches that seem
the winter's ashes, a wild Adam's unhappy maze,
a wicked world's answer to its doubt-ridden days;
against a mist like that within a dream,

and with a clarity that seems unreal,
like objects viewed but unheard, through a windowpane,
gold buds and emerald leaves sing again of our pain
in re-learning, through the risen Son's warmth, how to feel.

As dogwoods madly foam forth their milky froth,
as redbuds spray and spew their vintage rosé,
scattered, lake-like sky-blue puddles display
the heavens' image, mirrored on the earth.

William Ruleman

111. EASTER IN THE PUEBLO

You who this day arose
out of the cave's stale murk – the story goes –
and leaving tell-tale on the ground
your shroud and cerements unwound,
ascended to the white
kingdom of everlasting light,

bless my dark unbelief,
my spirit masterless, my uninstructed heart
that will not lift
out of its cleft of clay, or make a shift
to grow away from grief,
or, fearing greatly, set its fears apart;

and if I have no hope to rise
into that everlasting paradise
pledged with your ancient gift of wine and bread,
let a brief earthen jubilee be mine,
this tipsy festival that turns my head –
the clustering prattle of the flame vine,
hibiscus trumpeting, the glow
of bougainvillea like a purple snow,
bright oleander's brag; but most of all,
and truest to this time, the plangent fall
of the jacaranda, violet-blue,
heavenly blue, Sir, as your mother's shawl.

Such wantonness may bring me near to you.

Walter Nash

112. THE CRUCIFIERS

We killed "God's son" this afternoon
(some would say by mistake)
others, out of resentment over
changes that he would have us make

in our self-contained and fretful lives.
The funny thing is, he forgave us for it –
an act that drove some insane
for the sheer lack of logic in it.

By evening the show was over.
Some lingered near the scene
as over a job doubtfully done,
but most sought suitable shelter,

confiding their doubts to none
though quite willing to offer by phone
the scoop on what others wore
and who stayed distastefully late.

William Ruleman

113. ON THE VIA DOLOROSA

Likely more people there today
than then. Some carrying their cameras,
others imitations of the Cross,
carriers changed over just as
originally.
        Pushing past
the stations up the narrow suq
to where we turn after the steep
steps, the cross-bearer struggling
to gain the temporary flat,
confronted by two armed soldiers,
automatic weapons in the crooks
of arms, watching the processions.
        Over two millennia some
things never change –
except the technology of dying.

(Ed: A suq is an Arab market)

A.K.Whitehead

114. WHILE IT WAS YET DARK

This was the blackest night
since day and night first came.
After the grief that had shaken
even the Earth's frame,
now all was silent, bare;
beast and man alone, forsaken,
while hell was harrowed.
Only one ember alight
under the snows of despair.

Faith could not bridge death's chasm;
the followers stood weeping,
from all they had given, humbly,
ruin and derision reaping,
without understanding; hope slain.
With love still, they went early
while it was yet dark
and found Him risen,
yet did not know Him again.

In hope's cold entombment,
borne without bitterness,
hides still the seed of resurgence.
Out of the deep of the darkness
flowers the rose, grown
from disaster's quiet acceptance.
New, with swift exquisite life,
from the grave comes fulfilment
but first as a stranger, unknown.

Susan Glyn

115. THE COMFORTER

I am assigned, wherever you may go,
to be your servant and your enemy,
the measure of your gifts for good or ill,
your grief, your fear, your hopelessness, but still
your comfort, though you may not care to know
or honour me.

Men rack their lives for whispers of success
and in the consequence discover them
false, broken promises that wound their peace.
Prisoned in will, they fret for their release;
I visit them, and from their weariness
deliver them.

"Achievement" is their faith – the word implies
the toil of self to build a cave of air;
leave that illusion in a midnight wood,
repair to light, construct a quietude,
and listen, while I teach a way that lies
out of despair.

Your time is short, under a cooling sun,
to use the talent set aside for you;
begin a betterment, invest your days
in love's increase, in wonderment and praise,
and live for me, as I am sent by One
who died for you.

Walter Nash

X All Things Bright And Beautiful

116. GRACE

Sweet with a hint of corruption,
The blooming May has touched

The realms of light, A distant cuckoo
Activates the air – where blue

Is the reflection of an eye
That's glazed with spring. This is the prime

That fuses my emotions –
When blackbirds are the pose

That turns to song and campion
Have pinkened in my mind. Dampness

Was the dawning and the dew
Before the sun perused

The greening land and dried the tears
Of winter with its gold. Here

Is a remembrance and a dream –
An innocence that seems

To be revived and points towards
A pure, purported future.

The 'Golden Age' endures:
Enumerates the flowers in the sward –

And cancels time. There could be peace:
Just listen to the trees –

The sighing wind that susurrates,
Survives – and all is grace.

Martin Linford

117. EARTH'S RISING

It's the black muck of the bogs,
oozed from the ages of trapped suns, so far below,
when our earth sucked in light, so long ago,
then buried forests into fossil logs,
whose particles make the pure prismatic blue,
as the sun's rays draw moisture back to sky
in rainbows, signs that Heaven is not a lie.
Telling us that the Risen Body is true.

Susan Glyn

118. DYNASTIES

Great grown dynasties of trees
dwell peaceably in our policies
solitary or in families;
like generations of our elders,
placid, large, mysterious,
inhabiting our dreams and days.

In still nights of high summers,
denser than the darkest skies,
they move to tides of other airs,
huge vegetable presences,
remains of older dynasties
who once were lords of land and seas.

In their innocence, unawares
of the calculating gaze
of the lowest life in the ooze,
that would become the master race;
as we also now, for who knows
what next a grieving God may choose.

Our saving grace is that we learn
to love where there is no return;
our cross is God-like to look down
and see ourselves in space and time,
what once we were and shall become,
who out of Eden have no home.

Laurie Bates

119. WILD WOOD

The crows rake the air with sound and pursue
the ground for waste and trash; the thrilling
robin is rash with song and breaks out
throbbing dash and dot to warn the throng
of magpies in the yew and plane, that he
belongs where the drake and hen are fast,
in the glade where the willow and the alder stand.

The land is brown and red and gold in the bold
display of autumn; the lake is over-flowing
with animals that will migrate to west or south
in the colder months of winter, when
light and warmth are lost.

The habitat is busy with the burgeoning of berry,
nut and fruit; the harvesting squirrel is found
near the root of oak and elm; the land
is thriving in the fall of flower to seed,
to restore the field to beauty next spring.

The noise of God may seem like this, the hurrying
synthesis of work accumulating; the break
of winter with its quick and silent killings
makes all this business the more thrilling.

Bruce James

120. THE WINTER TREE

Beaded with blossom, hung with haggard leaves,
a symbol of this winter, come so late
that bulbs thrust up thin fingers to the cold.
Will hope that comes so premature to birth
speak to the darkened earth?
A world not ready yet to welcome him
still leaves the homeless poor outside the inn.

Joan Sheridan Smith

121. FEBRUARY'S FINAL FLING

What a morning this is!
Waking in bright light
believing we have overslept
to discover at least an inch of snow
on the balcony, footprinted and ruffled
by the first bird.

Snow lying along Winter boughs
on roof and gate and fence
on every little ledge
a moment of harmony
between nature and man's design.
Bushes we passed unheeding yesterday
Now outlined, glistening
In the rising sun.

By bell-raising
much of it will be gone
but children bound for Sunday school
will find enough in shaded places
for snowballing fun,
blowing on aching hands.

And I tread carefully
hoping, willing it to last awhile.

Sally Grey

[Bell-raising: the "turning up" of bells in the church tower – the bell is poised
mouth upward – ready for the ringers to begin a peal. This Sunday School is held
at 10am every Sunday.]

122. SPRING

I went out and I was seized with dread.
The Archangel of Spring was there,
bestriding my garden.
And I bowed my head.

The force of that upthrust
of unstoppable, invincible might
was cracking the winter earth;
driving shoots up to the light.

The incessant rain,
- late winter of snow and cold -
disappeared, helpless and vain.
A rearguard which couldn't hold.

Against the great power which burst
- asserting its right of passage –
"When the world was born, I came first."
The birds knew that winter was gone.

Then the Spring's earthquake began:
and I trembled and prayed,
finding no place for Man
in this violence and holiness of green.

If we come to another world,
we'll find a new Springlike scene.
But there we can greet it with joy,
and meet Archangels without fear.

Susan Glyn

123. WOOD SORREL

Late May, the day after Trinity, and a fine clear evening after rain:
I am walking the old path the miners walked
down from the high places into the dark wood.
The peat springs back beneath my feet,
the amber sun lifts my heart,
and I have seen the valley through buzzard's eyes
atop those jumbled rocks.
Now my boots are treading down between the larches,
and I brush against the berrywhin
as I make for the road and home.
Suddenly, where the path turns almost back upon itself
the woodland floor has become the night sky
so studded with stars it takes my breath away.
Closer, I see there are hundreds of flowers,
each one single and alone:
the white and delicate sorrel has taken sole charge here,
and every flower is love lit amid the darkness,
every threefold leaf a hymn to God.

William Rowell

124. LANDSCAPES

Along the lane in the late afternoon
hemmed in by thorns, all at once a gateway
opens a view of the far countryside.
Irregular grass fields with single trees
holding mist between overgrown hedges,
slope to thin lines of willow and alder.
Beyond the hollow, rough-grazing with gorse
rises to dark green-feathered felt of firs,
pulled well down on the brow of the hill.
Over all, cushioning infinity,
dove-grey flocculence of slow heavy skies,
vacant save low at the limit of sight,
a flock of birds like thrown seed wheels as one
and heliographs the last of the light.
All is silent and still, late afternoon
indeterminate time of year between
winter and spring, and countryside in mist,
withdrawn half-wild and overcast.

These are the landscapes we have always known,
original imprint of childhood scenes
engraved and beloved by lifetime bonding,
until the land itself seems sentient.
Now heart and eye run on in front with joy
and lo! The wanderer comes welcome home.
Released from motion thought or misgiving
and rapt between the silent earth and sky,
we sense the secret life of root and loam;
the almost sleep, the blessed breathing peace
of that other older natural world;
the lost divinely ordered universe
where humankind once dwelt and was content.
But where, though the exiles may revisit
on rare sabbaticals, they may not stay.
Already light fails and our clouded eyes
no touch can heal, see no longer the trees
standing, like gods in our lost paradise.

Laurie Bates

125. STEPPINGSTONE, YUKON

Where the Pelly joins the Yukon
there's beauty all rivers distil
if left in peace.
The gold-trail, long since left by man,
is walked now by a solitary bear,
hunching his way to watch the river,
read the salmon-runs
where moose browse knee-deep in the reeds.

Across the sky
sand-birds scoop mosquitoes,
flecking the air in jabs of light
to skim the river clean.
Life holds its balance here exact –
it wears its soul out-side.

John Waddington-Feather

126. MORTALITY

The flower head has fallen
short-lived and frail,
onto the harsh and adamantine
prehistoric stone;
the perma and the ephemeral.

Aeons to create the stone,
Time's own abacus,
and aeons its life-span:
but sand on the desert strewn
when die it must.

It is the flower's frailty
by which it will survive;
it has married mortality
and learned to die
so it might live

Laurie Bates

127. DANDELIONS

Humble dandelion, gold then white,
your mid-day blooms outblaze the sun
and then outshine the moon,
till windblown in time
you scatter galaxies of suns and moons
into a universe of fields.

John Waddington-Feather

128. SQUIRRELS AND STARLINGS

(for Mary Codd)

And God created Squirrels
Who run in Hertfordshire gardens,
Move softly to the house
Sunlit, through mint beds
Warmed in May green,
Peering through Wallflowers'gold,
Lithe on apple branches,
Foot noisy along fence tops
To the leafed Elms.

And God created Starlings
Trapped in neighbour's loft,
Crashing against fixed pane,
Pressed through the dark
To the roof space.
Journey of no return
And no continuance
Only the unrelenting pane
To waste wing strength
And light a Spring death.

John L. W. Robinson

129. MELOES*

They are shiny and black and clean
and they do no harm,
congregate if left alone
on yellow flowers, do not roam
unless you bring sweetpeas indoors,
when they make for the windows,
for the light one might suppose.

No surprise at all to find
one had fallen in the drink,
oaring valiantly round and round
between the swim and the sink;
no way he would escape that I could see
so I lifted him out and set him free,
as I were God and the beetle me.

Not to make a sermon out of the trivial
- except for him, trivial it was not -
but admire the insect instinct for survival,
we may need yet;
something inborn too long unused we must find
to bear the baggage of mankind,
the heart and the soul and the mind.

Laurie Bates

* pron. "meal-oes": fam.variant of "meal beetles"

130. AT THE AIR SHOW

From the long ancestry of evolution,
some element comes down to us from *birds*.
Race memories, perhaps of long-lost eagles,
never expressed in words,
are giving us recurrent dreams of flying.

We use our utmost skills, forever trying
to imitate the flight of flocks of birds.
Never attaining
their wheeling grace, the stillness of their planing;
that mystic understanding
which holds them, never touching, in formation;
guiding them as they curve and turn for landing.

In another world, where future and past can meet,
we may join our older selves, free to wheel round
in an infinite sky. Our innocence re-found
and life complete.

No sonic bangs, no smoke, no flaming crashes.
No Icarus in ashes,

Susan Glyn

131. SHADOW SHAPES

Summer will end now.
The craneflies are patterning,
pattering my lamp all night.
They skitter the ceiling,
dart at hair and eyes.

Betrayed by light,
some fizz in sacrifice,
or fly a fool's game,
across and across my room.
Rainsmoke swirls outside;

the old harp of chimney
and window frame plays
requiem. Yet two craneflies
settle beside me.
Quivering in delight

they mate, shadow shapes
matched in fragile elegance.
Even as death is preparing,
desire holds them, insists on
another year, another generation.

Pauline Kirk

132. dolphin dawn

Emerged from the silver sea
    a hump of bestial beauty,
levitating a moment between
    aquatic and aerotic worlds
then brimming face, puggy and serene
    pushing a glow into everywhere dark –
before taking a quick breath of light
    and plunging into invisible.

Though the rest of the day was gray,
    I breathed lighter,
thinking how close I got to God.

Philip Wesley Comfort

133. THE WALL

This ancient wall has seen so many summers:
sun sparkles now on quartz grains in the stone
as I sit here to take the valley view,
the climbing oaken hillsides and the river.

The busy hum of insect life around me,
makes clear these sterile rocks have come to life;
and the delicate spleenworts, purple toadflax,
valerian red and brash yellow of corydalis,
are quick to exploit the fissures that the years have made.

Consider this: that though the summer's warmth
makes this wall now a bright and busy place,
it was the winter's sharp and frosting blade,
the blast of storm wind, sweep of rain and snow
that brought these stones to what they are today,
that opened up the ways to let life in.

William Rowell

134. THE POOL

The small ornamental pool
at the corner of the lawn,
the dark bottle-green hole
defined by natural stone,
is a lens to focus vision
on this wet summer afternoon.

Slowly the raindrops fall
and slowly swells the ripple,
as the genius of the pool
performs kinetic miracle
unrolls its liquid skin
and puts it seamless on again.

The fish and the lotus flower
float between the stone,
symbols of life and colour
like those shards that stain
the green gloom of the windows,
with holy images and haloes.

Neither water now nor glass
but a window to the cell,
wherein not as prisoners
joyfully we dwell:
where free of worlds we are at peace
and in confinement find release.

Laurie Bates

135. THE WILD BUNCH

At the edge of the run-down town
unowned, uncared for, derelict,
bring the green life back again
rough and ready, the Wild Bunch moves in:
Ragwort, Rye Grass, Weld, Medick,
Fireweed, Vetch, Burdock and Rocket;
'Wilderness Rules O.K.' – all-star epic.

But the good times always pass away;
they do not last, for wild and free
is a fragile, fleeting thing,
too soon our young yesterday;
frontier ever moving, time flying,
green leaves of summer and all the flowers dying.

Bricks and mortar and the years bury us,
chequer-board checkmate of house and lawn
fence us in, no guns along these borders,
unsuitable mates side-lined,
the wild bunch boot-hilled, run out of town,
only the names and the legends remain
and the dormant seed deep down.

Laurie Bates

[Ed: "boot-hilled", from "boot hill", in Wild Western lore, the graveyard, outside the town
limits, and in unconsecrated ground, of the gunmen who "died with their boots on"]

136. THE YOUNG TREE

Its new leaves shake in the spring wind,
The sun leans its ambers on their planes –
The blue-tit shapes its ballets and dances
Upon its thin boughs; it houses the robin and the chaffinch,
And parades of sparrow pinch at its blades and stem.

The emblem of sorrow and pain regaining life eternal
The joys of its purpose spread out over the soil,
And its shades lessen the spoiling heat on the tulip
And rose, to break the seasonal cost of drought,
To come out and hold the rain.

Where else shall its divine origin express its roots
But here? The cell of its beauty spreads on this earth
Where Christ spent out his oaths and loves. Here He shapes
A future token of His memory; the limbs of His reason
Making this young growth bestow a welcome truth.

Bruce James

137. PATHWAYS

It's been a bad day.
Early October frost
has dribbled away the
clinging remains of autumn,
and the north wind carries
in its teeth the first
cold husks of winter.
Naked trees have filled
the drains with dying
leaves, and the roses lie dead
on pale bleached roads.
A hanging mist has
swirled away the day
and its touch still
lingers into the closing
darkness, stifling a
relief of stars.
The light from the house
sparkles a final blaze
on crystals clutching to
threads of grass as I
close the door on the
night, and let sprinkled
salt and my prayers
clear a pathway to morning.

Idris Caffrey

138. DANCERS

Calm and quiet September scene:
acres of stubble gleaned of grain,
evening sun more glow than shine,
bonfire's valedictory plume,
bitter-sweet scent for Autumn
and all the summers we have known.

The river is noiseless, and serene
an unnoticed passage of time,
and ever moving seems the same:
and here the handsome tall trees lean,
to print the waters' silken screen
with leaves to keep them ever green.

Now in the river, a whirlpool
small on its face as a dimple,
pirouettes alone and playful,
and soon assembles a quadrille
of flotsam, such as might travel
the waters, movers who never settle.

So happy and carefree they dance
it seems like destiny not chance;
one slips away and all at once
no trace of revelry remains;
only the loss of love and friends,
and bitter-sweet scent of summers' ends.

Laurie Bates

139. WARM RAIN

I see no reason
to shelter from this rain –
hide away beneath the white hawthorn.

There is so little to it –
just a fine spray like mist
that seems to have no purpose

but to invite us into its warmth
and then watch as it slips off leaves
to be swallowed by the growing earth.

The taste resting on lips,
wetness feeling for our cheeks
reminding us of lost tears
and how quickly we forget to cry.

Idris Caffrey

140. TOWPATH

The loom weaves slowly on
Pick by pick; to ease
My own breath, I step
Out, to the towpath.

Life is advancing, death
Is in suspense: a fishing rod
Poised across the water, a boy
Lounging beside it;

Ducks in loose formation, paddling
With strong feet towards Summit,
Breasting silver ripples like
The hammers poised to strike

The bell. They'll reach
And pass that window, its event
Waiting to happen…sent
For it, towards the future.

Robert Cockcroft

141. REMEMBRANCE DAY

Walk to the top of this gentle hill with me.
There! Do you see a rolling landscape
Patched with fields? Ribbed brown
Under the plough now, all harvests gathered.
But in spring and summer rich and ripe
With wheat and barley, Indian corn,
Lavender and shaggy sunflowers.

See, over there, on the fence post,
A carrion crow? Always hereabouts
The crow swoops and settles, shrugging
Down black wings.

These were the killing fields you know.
Over all these folded hills, armies marched,
Entrenched, filled the still air with noise
And smoke of shells, artillery battering.
The earth was ploughed with blood.
And no grass grew.
But the crow feasted; plenty of carrion then.

For years afterwards, the plough blade turned,
Brought up buttons and blades; small scraps
Of metal and leather, fragments of bone
The crow discarded.
Hard to imagine it all now, as winter evening
Flames and descends in scarlet silence. Hard
To remember those who should have led
The horse, driven the tractor, turned the plough;
Fragmented, buried, beneath their own good earth.

But always the crow flies here; generations
Of carrion crows perch on the fence posts.
Do you think they remember?

Rosi MorganBarry

XI Something For The Journey

142. COMMON PRAYER

In the sun after morning rain,
varnished wood in grain and colour,
the garden patio's paving stone
gleams like polished furniture.

Inside the house, out in the air,
this is our dwelling place and home;
patina of service, love and care,
tabernacle of wood and stone.

Sign and setting of our life here,
where hands have worked and feet have trod
in daily worship and common prayer,
inward and outward near to God.

Laurie Bates

143. GOOD COMPANIONS

The places we grew up in,
streets and houses and rooms,
trees and hedges, fence and garden
are childhood's setting
and our heirlooms.

That world we could touch and see
remains from long ago
and all the time and every day
we add to the repository
that stores our lives' scenario.

And when we recall our days,
not the first shout and show of life,
these faithful silent supporters
set the stage and properties
before the noisy ghosts arrive.

We have been consigned to care
for these friendly familiars,
good companions who daily share
our lives, our joys and hopes and fears;
it is from God, this bond between us,
that we God-like should love our creatures.

Laurie Bates

144. BRIDGE

The new road bridge was opened recently.
It combs the knots out of the traffic flow.
The river bulges here; across the countryside
the banks close in, yoked by a little bridge
that was not made for wheels.

A lane runs down, past houses and a church.
After the rood screen and misericords
you search out the path among the trees
leading to the medieval bridge.
No parapet occludes the downward view.
The water's bronze, with fry like blown pellets.
Upstream are mattresses of watercress.
Women once rinsed their linen at the brim.
In season now is lady's smock instead,
yellow flag, mint, balsam and meadowsweet,
flickering like print curtains in the wind.
Grey wagtails nest close by the riverbank.
In autumn there's a drift of crimson leaves.

On the farther side, the Friesian cows
come down to drink and stare; a Dutch master
would think himself back near his Haarlem home.
Beside the field's a fence; a green lane cuts
past more farmland, all part of an estate,
abbey lands under the Norman kings.
Packhorses carried salt and grain,
tallow and wool, barrels of ale and fish,
parchment and paints for the scriptorium.
Poor folk who'd had a blessing with their bread
cursed Thomas Cromwell when he came this way.

The new bridge stretches, steel nerved.
High-sided vehicles drive over it.
The old bridge is an irrelevance.
The river as a boundary's been rubbed out;
in drought a set of stepping stones would do,
and children don't play Pooh sticks any more.
Yet somehow you're at peace, standing there,
and no one uses it for suicide.

Isabella Strachan

145. TRANS-EUROPE EXPRESS

I shoved and pushed the whole way up the train.
Then leant out, looking at the view ahead,
so intent on it that I lost count of time.
A tunnel blocked it out, and I walked back.

But everything was changed.
"Where is the breakfast car?"
"They took that off at Basle."
I went down; saw nothing but strange faces.
"But where's the coach I had?"
"That went off hours ago."
"That was my seat!"
"You didn't buy the train."
"You're in the other section now, going to Budapest."
"But my ticket says Milan."
"That isn't valid here. No one can read that print."
The signs flashed past the train, incomprehensible to me.

They squashed up, giving me a seat.
"Never mind, mate. Come and enjoy the trip."
One of them shared a cup of beer with me.
An old man said, "That's life! You just go where you're sent.
Nothing belongs to you – except the ride."

Susan Glyn

146. WONDER

I was born,
opened my eyes
and wondered.

I started school,
opened my mind
and wondered.

I went to College,
opened my intellect
and wondered.

I was born,
opened my soul
and wandered.

Raymond Leonard

147. DO IT – JUST DO IT

If you can make a difference
Make it – make it.

If you think you have light
Let it shine – shine.

Love one another,
yes, love one another
as I have loved you.

When we love each other
the world will know
that the Father has sent me

I died for them, and rose again
so go – show – teach all nations
follow me as I follow God.

This is my commandment:
If you love me,
Do it – just do it.

Jerry Nicklas

148. WHO IS MY NEIGHBOUR?

I haven't got time...
    to see you
        read your article
            review your book
get a job for your godson
    find your mother a flat
        get you off the hook.

Because I've *had* my time
    My time ran out.
        I've been a has-been
            since a while ago.
The high-ups just look through me.
    But it mustn't get about.
        You mustn't know

I never did have time
    for hangers-on and spongers,
        people on my back;
            people like you.
It took me all my time
    to make it through:
        paddle my own canoe.

But then there came a time
    when I began to crack,
        felt myself slipping;
            went into free fall
I grabbed at anything
    trying to climb back.
        - No hand held out at all.

Susan Glyn

149. SAMARITAN

From the living thoroughfare
I looked into the graveyard,
and envied the people there
buried safe inside.

The clock struck from the tower
and mugged me where I stood;
it fell with such a power
I thought it struck me dead.

Silence after the final stroke
stretched taut as my life-line,
and then the fingers on the clock
jolted like guillotine.

The living passed heedless by;
the dead released their breath
and they made room for me,
sure it was my death.

So far gone and near to fall
I hung upon a thread,
and I could not to save my soul
move or speak a word.

God sent a common man my way,
he found me helpless in his path
and without malice jostled me,
and cursed me back to life.

Laurie Bates

150. YOU DON'T CARE WHAT PEOPLE THINK?

You ought to care what people think of you,
That's no excuse for living recklessly;
You're not alone in adding two and two.

You say it doesn't matter *what* you do
But *who* you are that counts; but I reply
You ought to care what people think of you;

Whether they're those who fly when you pursue,
A fact you won't forget, although you try
(You're not alone in adding two and two),

Or stand their ground, inviting you to view
The calculator in your neighbour's eye,
You ought to care what people think of you.

Alphabet soup can be a devil's brew
Wherein the toxins swiftly multiply
(You're not alone in adding two and two),

Unless it spells out something kind and true;
So use the spell-check others can supply.
You ought to care what people think of you;
You're not alone in adding two and two.

Robert Cockcroft

151. WITH A SIGHT DISABILITY AND LOW BLOOD SUGAR

Is there a diner or a café toward the bottom of the road?
Trust me to scout for one.
A pause and some refreshment raises mood.
Emergent colours are good too;
Chartreuse, tangerine, ice blue
(light blue that is bright as near white).

Here, neon signs, there, high heeled shoes,
The sources of my sight mimic
A metropolis of colour,
Of vibrant colour in disorganised complexity.
Nebulous neutrals dampen me down;
Dull battle-ship grey doesn't fire or sway:
They play like pale "Hellos" and "How are yous?"
From skint souls who see only damage.

But it's me!
I'm the person at the café by the end of the road
Sipping sweet expresso as I go.

Dorothy Koenigsberger

152. BRAVE AND BOLD

In the mid-morning sunshine
in this small bygone country town,
a young girl sits on a low brick wall
in a passageway just off the main street,
with a skeletal push-chair with straps
and a baby in it, with harness and bonnet;
a poke of chips in her trousered lap
and a cigarette held high and sideways
to keep the smoke out of his eyes.

She pushes her face at him and growls
as if to bite, he wriggles and gurgles;
then slowly, as if for her next trick,
selects a single chip, holds it up
and then poof! into her own mouth it goes,
at which he howls and throws himself about;
mock rueful, she shakes her head and sighs,
retrieves the chip intact
and pops it into his mouth whilst he still cries;
at once he kicks and crows, ecstatic
at the greasy morsel and the conjuring trick.

And so until the picnic ends,
when she stands up and shows her empty hands,
announces, 'All gone: that's it!'
and with one practised heave
sits him upright, strides briskly off
jouncing on the rough road
into their future brave and bold,
the two of them against the world.

Laurie Bates

153. PHARISEE

Invalids of Faith
yearn for health;
soul's sweet bonus
not for us.

We make do
with outward show,
decent public display,
rite and rote conformity.

Busy at bazaar stalls,
formal at funerals,
sidesmen at services,
patrons of empty pews.

We have paid
to Caesar and to God,
confessed our sin,
love our fellow men,

But we lack Faith
and neither lief nor love,
nor heart nor mind nor will
can overcome atrophy of soul.

Unease of half-belief,
malaise of unworth;
between would-be and is,
no bridge, no choice.

Learn then to live
neither without nor with;
pro-tem Pharisee –
God's wannabee.

Laurie Bates

154. THE LIFE OF MAN

Soon after marriage, his interest
(and the wife not always best pleased)
returns to men friends, bonding
in Orders or Clubs of good standing
where they meet and refresh and discuss,
and formally transact a little business;
except to belong, no other reward,
known and held in the members' regard.

And at the end, outside the Church
a group will stand near the West Porch,
Now apart, dressed in decent black,
come to pay their last respect,
man to man, each to another,
bearing a wreath from their Order:
'In memory of a Friend and Brother'.
And he would ask no higher, no other

Laurie Bates

155. THE TWO SHALL BE ONE

He loved her for her ironing,
and the way she washed the curtains every Spring.
Or so he said
to his mates in the village pub.

She loved him for his gardening
and his work in the potting shed.
Or so she said
to her friends at the women's club.

After too many beers
he would shed manly tears
about pride in his wife
and her hardworking life.

After too many years
all alone at the sink,
she looked older, and sad,
and complained she felt bad -

Which made some people think:
"Do those two share a bed?"

Susan Glyn

156. MEMORY'S DANCE

Major intensive events
occur sporadically,
happening only after
much thought
and preparation

Graduation days,
university,
getting married,
or the passage
of lifelong career.

In hindsight, memory
trivializes our recollections;
collective
in presentment.

Fifty, sixty, seventy years
of nostalgia
reduced to seconds.
Once hosts, we become
mere guests.

Paul Truttman

157. UNCLE CHARLIE

You never knew your Uncle Charlie:
he was my eldest brother,
a sergeant, killed in 1916
In some big battle that summer.

On his last night on leave,
they would have us all go
to the Nag's Head to see him off,
not that I wanted to.

Noise and smoke and heat
and songs about the war,
I couldn't stand it,
I said I'd have to go

He came outside with me
into the air – it was
a beautiful night in May
the sky full of stars.

He kissed me and said,
"It's goodbye this time, Nance,
you won't see me again,
I shan't come back from France."

He put a sovereign in my hand
and pressed the fingers down.
"There's a keepsake, Nance.
for when I'm gone."

I kept it till the Lock-out
in 1926, when we were clammed;
no money, nothing to eat.
Charlie would understand.

Laurie Bates

(ed: Clammed – northern dialect for 'hungry')

158. FOR ONE SHOT DOWN

'Angels ever bright and fair,'
he had sung when I was there.

Later the war, a sudden meeting,
unexpected, unexplained, a greeting
on a distant western prairie train
speeding amidst the harvest grain.
Later still, near the end, was heard
shot down over Holland,
the final word.

I thought of his singing
that song, that air,
'Take, O take me to your care.'

Where once we had sung,
a ruined shell,
I remember yet
where sky fires fell.

John L. W. Robinson

159. HOLY CITY

Jerusalem is where, seeking, I find you;
not in the dusty pathways of sacred history,
nor the narrow streets clogged with gunmen and pilgrims on
the move,

But where your presence transfigures
wilderness and grace,
and makes a Jerusalem place.

I recall your presence in the comforted yesterdays,
so glad that you were there then.
I saw your face.
But in the daily dying and the going on is my
Jerusalem place.

David Grieve.

160. NEW YEAR'S DAY WALK

We emerge at last from our hiding,
past the houses on the estate
to find that narrow lane
and our memories of nature once again.

      Tall factories hide
      behind thin trees;
      the hum of a motorway
      comes heavy on the breeze

We wind that path outside life's glare
on this first day of New Year,
to find holly berries as red as blood
and a World we try hard to love.

Idris Caffrey

161. THE LAST FAREWELL

After your car, your daughter and your wife,
(whichever order you may put them in),
there's still the parting with your life,
your body, which has been your friend.
Adding a lot to pleasures, sharing knocks,
and seeming to deserve a better end
than sending for scrap, in such an ugly box.

After a lifetime, no handshake, no pension.
Just to be left, fighting in bitter tension
against dismissal. What a breach of trust!
Peace only heals you when you come to terms -
promise the immortality of dust,
the other ticket to life, beyond the worms,
but not on the same train. It's still goodbye.

Susan Glyn

162. THE SUM OF THE PARTS

I've sent myself forward, luggage in advance,
one package at a time,
to an unknown station.

First it was my legs,
and then my strength.
But I was still here then,
still being *me.*

Then there was more to send:
my sight, my memory, my taste.
And almost all my breath.
Still I was *me.*

At last it was my mind. I felt it go.
It all meets up, I know,
parts re-assembled, living.
But now I don't ask <u>where</u>,
but Who I'm going to find.

Susan Glyn

163. LOVE

In the first flush of youth
in love with love and life,
the sweet pink girls with their wide eyes
and hearts of gold and wish to please;
and time flew by, became the years
before the War, the last of peace.

Enlisted then to the Wars, and found
comradeship and the lifelong bond:
never to be alone again,
fraternity of fellow men,
giving and gaining life in theirs,
with them and with ourselves at peace.

And then there came the love of God:
the unrequited aching need
that gives no peace and will not go,
the quest for what we do not know;
and may not be found
this side the grave – or beyond.

Laurie Bates

164. SONG IN FLIGHT
(perpetuum mobile)

Go, meekly, lightly,
into the years,
the exile years,
earth on her spindle
turns, the stars brightly
burn and dwindle,
go, the wheels grumble
under the load
in the rut of the road,
in hazards and fears
go, gallant and humble
into the years,
winds in the width of heaven
roam, in fields flowers
bloom, gifts are ours,
go, swaggering, mild,
to us, to us is given
a Child, reconciled,
go, doubting securely,
on to an end,
go, meekly, lightly,
into the years,
go, meekly, lightly…

Walter Nash

XII Closing the Book

165. LATTERDAYS

The evening's quiet now the gale has gone,
like life when wildness is no more;
for now I see how fondly once I reached
for vanity in youth, those empty quests
that blinded me to Christ.

My soul now housed in body growing old ,
raggled by suffering time has wrought,
peeps through its shattered walls;
my strength in weakness grows
the nearer I draw home.

Leaving the past behind I glimpse the new,
standing on the threshold of my room with God.

John Waddington-Feather

166. BIRTH AND REBIRTH

How long a baby spends, waiting for birth.
Kicking about, just growing, and maybe thinking;
dreaming his life on earth.
And how long, as life ends, we wait for death.
Shuffling about, just knowing; while life is shrinking.
Feeling our failing breath.
Knowing so many things. Yet unaware
what privilege to find in this repose,
unharnessed from the world and all its care.
What essence to distil from many griefs?
            And no one knows
how to re-weave the shreds of our beliefs.
But griefs will be transmuted in clairvoyance.
To see, we need the eyes of our Redeemer.
What seeds may germinate then, from our experience,
which He will bring to life, in our next Spring?
Now we can change from sufferer to dreamer
and lean on Him, in this as everything.

Susan Glyn

167. THE PRODIGAL

They know, the sea and the wind:
The sea that wears its wisdom in the sand,
The wind that writes its philosophy on the waves;
The leaf has curled words, even the shell a whisper;
They are all wise but me.

Where did I lose Eternity?
Here in the woods of living?
In the splendour of fleeting moments?
In mortal fascination?
Oh, teach me wisdom, wind that writes on the sea;
Explain my sin, O sea, with your wordless thunder.

Heartbreaking bird, shaking summer down
From the fiery bough, how have you found the secret?
Why am I lost, knowing only the tears
Of your near-knowledge? Why is the kingdom barred
To the man who is a child in search of God?

Yet though you answer in a higher tongue,
I know the truth, and that the Kingdom waits.
I had strayed to the cities from the stars,
To prisons from meadows, seeking thought in stones
And Eternity in a smile;
But I am returned, the prodigal of soul,
Seeking the world I scattered, seeking the world
That was never lost by wind or sea or bird.

Pamela Constantine

168. THE TIMELESS WELL

I grew up in the past.
My mother was brought up by an aged Granny
who had smelt the slaveships
coming into harbour in Brazil.
My father, nearly sixty, had known Alice in Wonderland
as a child. He dressed me to match her.
Our house was a thousand years old (in parts),
and infested by rats. With two ghosts,
fading presences from a far-off time,
now noticed only by children.

I wasn't sent to school, and only met "suitable" boys.
None of them thought about their future.
(You can't see what doesn't exist).
They were all killed in the War.
So the Present, when I finally met it,
was a strange encounter.
And I was alone with it.

"You haven't got a clue," they said.
But the Past was my compass
and steered me through the rocks.
Perhaps I had learnt from the ghosts
that the Past could be cruel and cold.
So I wasn't sucked back into it.
Perhaps I had learnt from the Well
deep under the house
a knowledge of permanence;
that change is like weather; passing over, soon gone,
and not to be feared.
So I welcomed the Present
with an explorer's joy.

Susan Glyn

169. ONE RECENT SUMMER
(written in the 1980s)

A jet makes its home in a swamp,
A gun digs an early grave,
Someone learns how to save,
Fifty skulls are unearthed at a camp.

Some more of the ozone melts.
Computers catch a new virus.
Somewhere, a new cult of Osiris,
More bombing by angry Celts.

Thousands, somewhere, are weeping.
Yet the crime-rate's on the decrease
Will wonders never cease?
A mood of malaise goes creeping

over the lands, the oceans
underground, in the airwaves. . .
It's summer, and everyone craves
the latest sunscreen lotions.

The First Lady finds a soothsayer,
A hurricane rips off a coast.
Economy's better for most,
and who is kneeling in prayer?

William Ruleman

170. THE UNFOLDING

In the fellowship of the dying
we make our pilgrimage
towards the Holy.

More real to us now
than the stages of our journey
is the divesting of ourselves
of all the cloaks which life has wrapped around us.

As Our Lord surrendered
first the Purple Robe of power,
then His own seamless robe,
His garments, and finally the Body
which holds the Spirit within us,
so we unfold *our* layers.

Discarding strength, and all desire;
the crust and scars of our experience;
heredity, and its sub-personalities;
to bare our true selves.

An unfolding rose is beautiful,
as one by one its petals open, curl, then fall,
in a slow dance.
The centre it reveals is golden.

Susan Glyn

171. THE LAST CLIMB

And when I come to the path's end that now I tread
I hope and shall believe
there'll be revealed a new way I may follow,
that rinses through the rocks and scented heather
until before me I shall see the King's high throne,
and its curving walls of stone all fiery with the new dawn.

and in that place will be no more mourning or crying or pain,
only the buzzard's winged cry
and the dew-tears that scatter the grass at daybreak;

and I shall climb on and higher
to where cool mountain streams are fringed with stars of asphodel;
I shall walk in the clear air
where ouzel and curlew sing their alleluias;
and I shall step out onto those cloud-high places
and have no fear of falling.

William Rowell

172. ARCHIVES AND ANGELS

There were times of innocence –
green rivers leaping with trout,
lazy Summers hazy as dreams
and a mistaken belief
that this would last forever.
There were always journeys –
other places soon forgotten,
false escapes down grey roads
that went round in circles
and led back to the start.
There were times of loss –
Autumns as frail as love,
cast away by wind blown trees
and filling rooms with dying leaves.
Then there is today –
a morning sheeted in sun
and the sudden realisation
that how we have lived our lives
is what we have now become.
There were always angels
in the shafts of light
that came blazing through
the chapel's coloured glass,
in snow covered hedges
that rose high above the lanes.
There are still thoughts
of what might have been,
but in tomorrow there is hope again
with angels waiting in the wings,
ready and willing to draw me home.

Idris Caffrey

173. WAKING LATE

So I hope to have of Him that is Almighty
A gobbet of His grace, and begin a time
That all times of my time to profit shall turn
      - Langland, Piers Plowman

And beginning to feel too old for this, push away
   the warm clasp of the bedclothes, and emerge
fretful and gasping into the frozen light. Why,
   here I am again! New-hatched, on the wrinkled marge
of a heaven-sent day; soon to hobble on wry feet
   to the bathroom, urinate, wash, peer
at the gaunt white comedian (gumskull) challenging fate
   from the mirror's ghostly pale, my ghastly pair,
asking what plan for today, what goal of thought shall guide
   the aims of which our hopes shall not fall short?
Hopes! Well, as to that, I hope to serve God
   with a cheerful heart and a fairly clean shirt,
but even so, the devils of seventy mump and mock;
   for "hope", these latterdays, is less, I feel,
a divination than a dour precaution; pack-a-mac,
   not magnet; to be carried, without fail,
at all times, lest the heavens open, time called,
   and eternity arrive in a shower of remorse.

At seventeen, hopes were simple – simply not to be killed
   at the murderous whim of a raucous monster, Mars
the *Übermensch* with a moustache; but three more years
   and the case is altered. Bliss then, *bliss* indeed
in that dawn to be alive, and told, "the world is yours",
   you being most decidedly not dead,
but Billy College, clad in quotes and corduroy
   and plentiful conceit. Days garden-walled,
when expectation like a single, uninflected ray
   of warm light filled the borders of my world.
That was the time, beginning of beginnings, when

the moves of an enormous game looked
so enormously easy. How could one fail to win?
    The mind liberated, the heart unlocked
to begin the quest, hoping for wealth, and fame, and love -
    those sky-high fantasies, oh, draughts of wine
by pure Arcadian streams, poems dense as leaves
    in forests of owls, scarlet gown worn
with immense distinction, my name on innumerable lips -
    and even mentioned on "the wireless" – hopes
to be frustrated only by a disastrous lapse
    of taste on Destiny's part; barring mishaps
the road would surely run where Inclination lay.
    So tell me, reflective shade, where are we now?
The spectre in the looking-glass does not belie
    my fleshly fact. He tells me what I know -
singula de nobis praedantur anni euntes...Look!
    balding, edentulous, blear eye, shrunken calf -
aye, there you have it, Horace – and here's no lack
    of supplementary effects, the cough
that terrifies the night, the hip, the blight that stops
    at no indignity, shame of breaking wind
inappositely, dribbling, tumbling down steps;
    and conscience always twisting in some wound
that brings contrition home in the dark of half-past four.

    My time is nearly up. I have not set
the Thames, or any lesser watercourse on fire,
    or won a monumental prize, or sat
on buttoned leather or exultant shoulders. Poor's
    hardly the word, but *tight* – Horatian style -
the ample larder and the regulated purse,
    obliged to borrow, never to beg or steal,
always enough. *Satis*, and satisfied; but *sated?*
    No, nor wish it; I have known my fill
of such a love as leaves a deep devotion sited
    steadily in the heart, never to fail.
Sit mihi quod nunc est, my mister Horace says -

give me what's going, though the going rate
will very soon be gone. Each morning's glass foresees
    change in the tale of where we are; the route
ahead points to a terminus on that wheezing shore
    where hope is pointless and illusion lost.
Shave carefully, then… Try not to fall in the shower.
    It is time at length to begin to expect the last.

Once upon a time we talked about "despair".
    It occurred in books. We rather liked its style,
fancying its print in our commonplace lives, the spoor
    of a striped and silent menace (tyger) that stole
softly through our existences, behind the trip
    to Worthing, or the "do" for the junior staff:
despair, the brindled whippet, smart out of the trap,
    the right dog for a knowing lad. Such stuff!
Despair is harder going, worse than being bored
    or splenetic, or given to megrims. Let
me tell you, mirror, while you trim your goaty beard,
    what despair is. It is knowing you are too late
to change what has to be changed; that the peripatetic days
    have passed beyond your good intentions. Time
is shrinking into smaller segments. The will dies
    as perspective narrows. Hour by hour the term
of penitence and atonement squeezes tighter. How
    can I force this moment onto its little knees,
renouncing all beginnings past, knowing Who
    was there from the very beginning? God alone knows
my worst, then how shall I please him? With what fusty lore
    of things over and done, my this and thus
like snapshots of holiday pleasure, the *fun*, the vacant allure,
    the glasses raised, the grinning faces? *These*
foolish things remind me of you, Death; inert
    memorials of a fruitless time, torn
leaves from a frivolous album. Now let me study an art
    that all times of my time to profit shall turn,
crouched at the edge of the bed, one frayed sock in hand,.

let me attempt my prayers before I lose
what I was going to say. How the wit leaves behind
the what, old man. Somebody shut the gate
or the words will straggle out sad and empty to stare
speechless at the uncomprehending street.
Now is my time, high time, to begin to steer
a course for the ultimate, and steer it straight:

Master of mysteries, and King, long ages gone
taken thief-wise for torture on the Cross,
despatched to lie in earth all night, and so again
to rise, glorious, morning-hale; my crass
and uncreative days forgive. My spectre, black
against the light, dismiss. Let me cast off
the speculative shape that burdens, questions, blocks,
mocks, my life's meaning. Sir, if
you need pain from me, take it. If even my mind
must yield, break it: but do not withhold
your presence from my life. Almost too late to mend
the broken promise, getting far too old
for days like this, I own I cannot bear, Christ,
to be without you. Your bonded light -
spectrum of prayers – prisms my dark, the broken crust
of your body sustains me. Let it not be too late
to begin a time, in hope and cheerfulness, to taste
a draught of sweet wine at the very edge
of the last river, and sained in cleanliness, to test
your sheer truth in the shabby house of age.
And let these voices babbling in my heart devise
such songs, such leaping verses, that although
the verse falters, still the music makes your voice
my cry; and let my cry come home to thee.

Walter Nash

174. IN WHAT DEEP OF LOVE

In what deep of Love
His heart moves, sets the suns
to shift within. He dances,
spins and coils and whirls
the soul with grace,
until the ecstasy relieves,
and places stars within to play.

I know Him near as day,
as vital as the universal space,
through which He speeds,
and makes the boundaries of grace
appear as near as the air I breathe;
and, finding me dazed
from life's vain night, He heals me,
devises love, by which
He frees and leads me to Him,
secretly.

I span a heaven, rest sanctified
by his touch, and know such
favours of Eternity I feel
my soul aflame with love,
and reach up and see His face.
Where light of Light of light
appears, and all of me is satisfied,
and kindly, He sets me free
to see Him, as He is always.

I hold Him as a star might know
the firmament, secure and brilliant
in His grasp; the course of night
begins to flood away,
as days of Him recur until the soul
is fast and bright. Then, quickly,
as He came, he disappears,
apparently to hide within,
and stay secret, undefiled.

Bruce James

175. JERUSALEM

I live in a sphere.
My pattern is whole,
And the pattern within is the same as
      the pattern without.

The cupped dew
Has all the light
Of all the sky in its sphered surface.

Christ enthroned
Holds an orb
In his all-containing hand.

Caroline Glyn

176. PRAYER

Oh God, whose Love is free
yet sought by few,
in this world of pain
Renew the search for You;
and finding you are there,
always to be good,
remind us that You choose
to love infinitely.
Tender us, we pray,
what is beyond reason,
beyond life;
which feeds and fills us
whether we laugh or cry.
For you are loving,
in the invisibility of night,
and in the day
You are the one true Light.
Father, gather our selves in peace
before Your throne,
and for Your mercy's sake
never leave us, Lord, alone. Amen.

Bruce James

INDEX OF POETS AND POEMS

Number references are to poems as listed on the Contents page

REMEMBRANCES

Laurie Bates,   b.1918 d.2005, a distinguished, and in worldly judgement unrecognized, poet. He was born in the Midlands, son of a coal miner who was killed down the pit. In his poems, glimpses of his youth in the twenty years before the outbreak of the second World War suggest a young man diffident, searching for identity, hapless and uncertain in relationships. After wartime service (and the experience of comradeship) he moved north to County Durham, where he worked for the National Coal Board. There he became an active member of a famous and historic church, St.Mary and St. Cuthbert, Chester-le-Street – "awesome as henge and beautiful / as a tall ship under full sail". In this environment, and in the calm haven of his home and garden, he fashioned a faith, always firm though seldom without its doubts and questionings. His last years were shadowed by mourning for his wife, Dorothy, who died in 2001. He published eight collections of verse with Feather Books. His wish to be acknowledged was almost grievous. He admitted, in private correspondence, to sitting deep into the night labouring over intractable verses. This is not unknown among poets; in his case, the discipline produced an unmistakable style, at once closely formal and boldly eccentric.

Caroline Glyn, b.1947 d.1981. Daughter of the novelist Anthony Glyn and the artist and poet Susan Glyn, she was all her life estranged from the world, by her own brilliance and social backgound, as well as by a severe and disabling illness that eventually claimed her as she was scrubbing the kitchen floor of the convent she had helped to build in the Australian outback. She began writing poetry at the age of 4, and published her first poem at the age of 9 She published her first (best-selling) novel in 1963, at the age of 15, then between 1965 and 1973, a further six novels, three in the form of a trilogy. Shortly after completing the trilogy, distressed by an unspiritual world, she entered the closed life, as a novice in the Anglican order of the Poor Clares. She continued to write in the convent – stories, meditations, poems, always with the tendency of mysticism bred out of observation that characterises all her work.. She had studied art in Paris in the 1960s, and continued to use her gifts as painter and illustrator of religious themes. Feather Books have published two of her books posthumously: the collection *Chawton and Other Poems* (2000), and *Last Stories of Dream and Vision* (2000). There is a study of her poetry, and that of her mother, Susan, in *A Family of Poets*, by Walter Nash, (Feather Books, 2002)